Transition Costs of Fundamental Tax Reform

T0273263

Transition Costs of Fundamental Tax Reform

Kevin A. Hassett and
R. Glenn Hubbard

The AEI Press

Publisher for the American Enterprise Institute
WASHINGTON, D.C.

2001

Library of Congress Cataloging-in-Publication Data

Hassett, Kevin A.
    Transition Costs of Fundamental Tax Reform Kevin A. Hassett and
      R. Glenn Hubbard p. cm.
    Essays prepared for an AEI conference
    Includes bibliographical references
    ISBN 0-447-4111-6 (cloth   —ISBN 0-8447-4112-4 (pbk.

    1. Taxation—United States—Congresses. 2. Taxation—Economic
aspects—United States—Congresses. 3. Spending tax—United States—
Congresses. I. Hubbard, R. Glenn. II. Title.

HJ2381.H344 2001
336.2'05'0973--dc21

1 3 5 7 9 10 8 6 4 2

The AEI Press
Publisher for the American Enterprise Institute
1150 17th Street, N.W., Washington, D.C. 20036

00-029974

Contents

Contributors

ALAN J. AUERBACH is the Robert D. Burch Professor of Economics and Law and the director of the Burch Center for Tax Policy and Public Finance at the University of California, Berkeley. He is a research associate of the National Bureau of Economic Research. Mr. Auerbach taught at Harvard University and the University of Pennsylvania. He was a deputy chief of staff of the U.S. Joint Committee on Taxation in 1992. Mr. Auerbach is a fellow of the Econometric Society and of the American Academy of Arts and Sciences.

DONALD BRUCE is a research assistant professor at the Center for Business and Economic Research and an assistant professor of economics at the University of Tennessee, Knoxville. He specializes in empirical research in public finance and labor economics, particularly the economic effects of taxation. His recent work includes an investigation of the effects of rapidly expanding electronic commerce on state sales tax revenue.

WILLIAM G. GALE is a senior fellow and the Joseph A. Pechman Fellow in Economic Studies at the Brookings Institution. He is the coeditor of *Economic Effects of Fundamental Tax Reform* and of the *Brookings-Wharton Papers on Urban Affairs*. Mr. Gale was an assistant professor at the University of California, Los Angeles. He was a senior economist at the Council of Economic Advisers. He has written extensively on taxes, saving, and public finance.

KEVIN A. HASSETT is a resident scholar at the American Enterprise Institute. He had been a senior economist at the Board of Governors of the Federal Reserve System and an associate professor of economics at the Graduate School of Business, Columbia University. Mr. Hassett was a policy consultant to the Treasury Department during the Bush and the Clinton administrations.

JAMES R. HINES JR. is a professor of business economics and the research director, Office of Tax Policy Research, at the University of Michigan Business School. He is also a research associate at the National Bureau of Economic Research.

DOUGLAS HOLTZ-EAKIN is a professor and the chairman of the Department of Economics at Syracuse University; he is also the associate director of the Center for Policy Research at Syracuse. Mr. Holtz-Eakin is the editor of *National Tax Journal* and a member of the editorial board of *Economics and Politics, Regional Science and Urban Economics,* and *Public Works Management and Policy.* He has taught at Columbia and Princeton Universities. He was the senior staff economist at the Council of Economic Advisers in 1989–1990 and was a member of the Economics Advisory Panel to the National Science Foundation from 1996 to 1998. Since 1985 he has been a faculty research fellow and research associate of the National Bureau of Economic Research.

R. GLENN HUBBARD holds the Russell L. Carson Professorship in Economics and Finance at Columbia University. At the National Bureau of Economic Research, he is a research associate in programs on public economics, corporate finance, industrial organization, monetary economics, and economic fluctuations. Mr. Hubbard is also a visiting scholar at the American Enterprise Institute.

KENNETH L. JUDD is a senior fellow at the Hoover Institution on War, Revolution and Peace. He has taught at the Kellogg Graduate School of Management, Northwestern University, and at the University of Chicago. Mr. Judd researches taxation, imperfect competition, economic theory, and mathematical economics.

ANDREW B. LYON is an associate professor of economics at the University of Maryland. He has served on the staff of the Council of Economic Advisers and of the Joint Committee on Taxation and was a visiting fellow at the Brookings Institution. His current research includes corporate investment, the effects of taxation on portfolio choice, and taxation with informational asymmetries.

PETER R. MERRILL is the director of the National Economic Consulting Group for PricewaterhouseCoopers LLP, of which he is a principal. He is also responsible for the firm's Tax Technology Consulting, also in Washington, D.C. He had been the chief economist for the Joint Commmittee on Taxation of the U.S. Congress. Mr. Merrill had been a consultant to the National Economic Commission. He also was a lecturer at Harvard College.

He has advised the governments of Poland, the former Yugoslavia, the former Soviet Union, Bulgaria, and Russia on the reform and enactment of income and value-added taxes. His expertise includes international taxation and tax policy, financial services, electronic commerce, and energy and environmental tax policy.

1

Introduction

Kevin A. Hassett
and R. Glenn Hubbard

In 1986, congressional Democrats and Republicans came together to produce the Tax Reform Act of 1986, a sweeping reform that lowered marginal tax rates and broadened the tax base. Although many economists felt that the law, given its broad bipartisan support and sound economic underpinnings, would stand for many years, events soon proved them incorrect. Significant increases in marginal tax rates were passed in 1990 and 1993; subsequent reforms have narrowed the tax base and have increased effective marginal rates in a particularly crazy hodgepodge. The tax system is now probably further from the economic ideal than in 1985, and economists are again calculating and debating the potential gains to the economy from another fundamental tax reform.

Many fundamental reform proposals, such as Hall and Rabushka's flat tax or other forms of a consumption tax, promise economic benefits by lowering marginal tax rates and by changing the tax base to bypass those areas of the economy that are particularly costly if taxation distorts them. The key sector is capital formation, which has long and widely been acknowledged as especially impaired by taxation. Most economists concur on the potential magnitude of economic benefits from excluding capital from taxation.

But economists do not agree that a sudden switch to a consumption tax would be an obvious improvement. Many have argued that the severity of the problems of managing a smooth transition would preclude even contemplating such a change. In particular, the current tax system distorts behavior in many ways; yet the removal of those distortions would hurt those who played by the old rules. Building in transition relief to help those hurt most by the reform would diffuse the benefits of the reform. In their introduction, Henry J. Aaron and William G. Gale conclude that "the gains from realistic reforms may not be as large as advocates have hoped, and ... the process of adjustment to a new system will not be easy" (1986). By realistic, they mean reforms that would provide relief to the short-term losers. In many simulations presented in Aaron and Gale 1996, apparently reasonable transition relief often would almost completely exhaust the potential benefits of tax reform.

This volume has collected three essays prepared for an AEI conference on the transition costs of fundamental tax reform. Each chapter begins by relaxing a simplified assumption employed by the previous literature and proceeds to explore how the relaxation of that assumption affects the calculus of tax reform. The authors challenge the perception that we cannot get there from here in two ways. They suggest that the benefits of fundamental tax reform are likely to be significantly greater than previously believed and that the transition costs would be significantly less.

In chapter 2, "The Impact of Tax Reform in Modern Dynamic Economies," Kenneth L. Judd argues that tax reform analysis by and large has ignored issues of imperfect competition, risk, and human capital and has significantly understated the benefits from fundamental tax reform. Judd lays out the basic economics that underlies the claims that the current tax system is particularly pernicious to the national economy. Most important, he points out that a tax system that distorts the savings and investment decision causes a deflection that grows over time. Because even a small distortion becomes enormous over time, only a zero tax on savings and investment is optimal.

Our current system of taxation is clearly not optimal. But what would happen if we switched to a tax system that did not tax savings? To answer this question, Judd incorporates several important real-world features into existing models used to study tax reforms. The first is imperfect competition. Most models used for studies of tax policy assume that firms have no market power. In such a world, the market's competitive equilibrium in the absence of taxation would be highly efficient. If firms have market power, which seems likely, then the equilibrium in the absence of taxes is inefficient. Firms with market power increase profits by cutting back production. Introducing taxes in such a world would exacerbate existing distortions because the economy is already out of competitive equilibrium. Indeed, an optimal tax would *subsidize* capital formation to counteract the output reductions caused by the profit-maximizing firms. When Judd calculates the switch to a consumption-based tax in the presence of imperfect competition, he finds that benefits are much greater than previously forecast.

Judd then adds two layers of complexity. First, he incorporates risk. The current tax system discriminates against risk taking: risky investments that pay off are taxed, but losses do not lead, at least in all cases, to tax refunds. Second, he introduces the formation of human capital, which is important for growth but is taxed heavily when income taxes are steeply progressive. Each of these steps contributes significantly to Judd's measure of the gains from switching to a flatter consumption-based tax.

In his final section, Judd uses the lessons derived from the more general approaches to investigate the impact on the distribution of tax reform. The wage increases attributable to higher amounts of capital in the postreform economy would have an important impact on the distribution of the benefits of tax reform, but most analyses uniformly ignore this key point.

Critics of tax reform proposals often argue that lower capital taxation would lead to a stock market crash. The mechanism for that event would be quite simple. Because the reform would lower the cost of capital, new investment would create competition that would destroy the profits of existing firms. Compensating existing capital for such damage is a primary demand for transition relief. In the third chapter, "Asset Price Effects of Fundamental Tax Reform," Andrew B. Lyon and Peter R. Merrill question Judd's view.

Lyon and Merrill argue that a significant portion of the value of existing firms is attributable to goodwill and other intangibles. Value attributable to these assets would actually increase after a tax reform of the type considered here because the taxes on the future economic profits of such firms would be lowered. The authors demonstrate that even if firms did not have intangible assets, the effects on asset prices from fundamental reforms would be less than previously estimated if actual tax depreciation rules were used in the calculations, instead of the simplified patterns employed in previous research. Lyon and Merrill show that the effect on asset prices would be less if firms adjusted their capital slowly in response to the reform. Finally, they review empirical evidence from past reforms and conclude that stock prices have generally increased after fundamental tax reforms; that result confirms their analysis and undermines the case for transition relief to existing firms.

Owner-occupied housing is perhaps the most favored asset under the current tax system, with the deduction for mortgage interest the most lucrative tax benefit for most taxpayers. What would happen to housing prices if the mortgage interest deduction were removed? Many have argued that an Armageddon could occur in the housing sector. The demand for housing would plummet, and housing prices would follow suit. Transition relief for homeowners or the continuation of the current system of deductions for mortgage interest would be the other major complications to a transition. But would housing prices really drop after a tax reform?

Donald Bruce and Douglas Holtz-Eakin explore this issue in the final chapter, "Will a Consumption Tax Kill the Housing Market?" They develop a rigorous supply-demand model of the housing market and link the transitional and long-term impact of tax reform. Although some analysts have argued that declines in housing prices would be short-lived because housing starts would drop and thus lower the overall stock of housing capital, Bruce and Holtz-Eakin go a step further. In their setup, the elimination of the deduction for mortgage interest need not lead to a sharp decline in housing prices, even in the short run.

They present a simple, intuitive example for such a result. Suppose that the United States switched to a 20 percent national sales tax and—just to keep the example clean—nobody claimed the deduction for mortgage interest under the old system. When the sales tax went into effect, individuals would pay a 20 percent tax when they bought a new house, but no tax if they bought a "used" house. The price of "used" houses must then rise by 20 percent. Whether such an effect would be empirically important would, of course, depend on the magnitude of the effect on mortgage interest and the impact on the existing stock of housing. Bruce and Holtz-Eakin conclude that the two effects approximately cancel each other and that housing prices would probably not decline significantly after a fundamental tax reform.

Although commentaries on each chapter outline important qualifications, taken together the essays suggest that the case for transition relief to home-owners and firms may be weaker than expected. In that case, even if the complications explored by Judd were ignored, the gains from fundamental tax reform would be significant. If imperfect competition, risk, and the formation of human capital were also important real-world considerations, then the gains of fundamental reform might be even higher.

References

Aaron, Henry J., and William G. Gale. 1996. *Economic Effects of Fundamental Tax Reform.* Washington, D.C.: Brookings.

2

The Impact of Tax Reform in Modern Dynamic Economies

Kenneth L. Judd

S ince World War II, the tax policy in the United States has been based on the principles of an income tax. Its intellectual foundation lies in the Haig-Simons approach to the taxation of income: define income properly and tax it. However, economists over the past thirty years have increasingly argued for moving away from the taxation of income and toward the taxation of consumption. Debates on tax reform often focus on the choice between taxing income and taxing consumption

The key issue is the taxation of savings and investment.[1] Many theoretical analyses have argued for a zero long-run tax rate on capital income. Early arguments—such as those made by Feldstein (1978), Atkinson and Sandmo (1980), Auerbach (1979), and Diamond (1973)—relied heavily on assumptions of separability and on identical agents in each cohort. Judd (1985b) proved that the optimal long-run tax rate on capital income is zero even when tastes are not separable and when agents have different tastes and abilities. Others have explored taxation issues in models of economic growth. Eaton (1981) showed that taxation of capital income reduces an economy's long-run

I thank Alan Auerbach, Kevin Hassett, Glenn Hubbard, Alvin Rabushka, and participants of AEI's Conference "The Transition Costs of Fundamental Tax Reform" for their many useful comments. I acknowledge the support of NSF grant SBR-9708991.

growth rate; Hamilton (1987) demonstrated that the asymmetric treatment of different kinds of investment has a high efficiency cost. Judd (1999) generalized the Judd (1985b) analysis to include investment in human capital, government expenditure, and various forms of growth. All these analyses argue strongly against taxation of asset income in the long run.

Estimates of benefits to the economy from tax reform have supplemented the increasingly robust theoretical case against the taxation of asset income. Studies such as Jorgenson and Yun 1990 and Auerbach 1996 show that switching to consumption taxation would significantly increase savings and the labor supply and would improve productivity. Computed examples in Jones, Manuelli, and Rossi 1993 show that the effects on asset income should be minimal even in the intermediate run. Both theoretical and empirical work demonstrates that a pure income tax system is far from the best for aggregate output.

The U.S. tax system has evolved into a hybrid system combining features of income and consumption taxation,[2] but the corporate income tax and the limited nature of savings incentives still give the current system a strong income tax flavor. Most economists agree that moving completely to consumption taxation would improve aggregate productivity and income in the long run. Problems arise concerning issues of the transition process and distribution. Some critics have argued that considerations of equity and problems of transition related to changes in asset prices blunt the case for a complete move to consumption taxation and make it politically less viable. In particular, the elimination of many middle-class tax deductions reduces middle-class support for tax reform. Possible adverse impacts on asset prices may make some individuals, particularly the elderly, worse off than under the current tax system. Any debate on tax reform will consider the trade-offs between the long-run benefits and the short-run problems of transition.

This study examines the conceptual basis for a consumption tax and introduces many features of a modern economy that have been ignored in analyses of tax reform but substantially strengthen the case for switching completely to consumption taxation. Despite the theoretical literature, some authors (for example, Gravelle 1994) still assert that the efficient taxation of capital depends on the relative elasticities of consumption demand and the labor supply. This chapter reviews the theory behind the consumption tax and shows that the case against capital taxation and for consumption taxation is surprisingly robust and does not depend on unknowable, technical details of the economy. The conceptual foundation leads to other aspects of consumption and capital taxation, in particular the implications of adding imperfect competition, risky assets, and the formation of human capital to the standard analysis. Any analysis, including this one, must make many simplifications: ignoring those elements was natural for the initial analyses of tax reforms. Now that we understand the implications of tax reform in a competitive economy, we should extend our models and make them more realistic. It is natural to include imperfect competition, risky assets, and human capital in tax analysis—it is difficult to imagine a modern dynamic economy without these features.

Unsurprisingly, adding imperfect competition, risky assets, and human capital affects our results, but this study argues that incorporating these elements substantially strengthens the case for a consumption tax. First, including these elements of a modern economy materially increases the estimates of the gains to long-run productivity. Interactions between taxation and imperfect competition increase the welfare cost of income taxation. The current U.S. tax system discriminates against risky assets; this study shows that any tax reform that would eliminate this feature would produce significant gains in efficiency. Including human capital in the analysis increases the welfare gains from eliminating the taxation of income on new investment.

Second, the extra considerations reduce problems during transition. The incorporation of imperfect competition moderates, possibly even reverses, adverse movements in asset prices. That change, plus a detailed view of U.S. demographics, reduces the problems of protecting older individuals who may not live long enough to enjoy the long-run benefits of tax reform. The incorporation of human capital also suggests new ways, consistent with the principle of a consumption tax, to compensate the middle class for the elimination of current deductions.

Some basic ideas from public economics and industrial organization prompt those considerations. In particular, this study presents basic results from optimal tax theory, uses them to analyze the inefficiencies of conventional income tax, and discusses interactions between taxation and imperfect competition. The usual discussions focus on the distinction between income and consumption taxation. But there is no distinction between income and consumption taxation: income taxation is really a special pattern of consumption taxation. More precisely, income taxation is a particularly inefficient form of consumption taxation, one that violates basic rules for a sound tax system. The focus should instead be on the taxation of consumption today relative to consumption tomorrow and on the taxation of intermediate goods relative to final consumption goods. The change in focus helps to explain old results and to point in useful new directions.

First, many taxlike distortions exist in the private sector. When teaching competitive economic theory, economics professors often use the example of the hundreds of thousands of farmers producing an agricultural product and correctly argue that no individual producer has any impact on the price of his crop. Tax reform analysis usually employs this competitive paradigm. Although the competitive model may have been a valid simplification in 1800, it is certainly not in the modern industrial high-technology U.S. economy of 2000. Today imperfect competition and oligopolistic interactions provide a more appropriate description of much of the economy and are particularly appropriate when discussing capital goods and innovations that are sources of economic growth.

Parts of competitive theories still hold. In particular, competitive forces in oligopolistic sectors may reduce profits to competitive returns and prices to average cost. However, we expect prices to exceed marginal cost. The relationship between price and marginal cost, not price and average cost, determines efficiency and welfare. This wedge between price and marginal cost is essentially a tax, even when generated by the private economy.

This chapter shows that the presence of imperfect competition strengthens the case for consumption taxation because it increases the estimates of the aggregate gains in efficiency from tax reform. In fact, estimates of the discounted welfare gains from switching to a consumption tax are at least doubled for central estimates of the critical parameters, and the estimates of the long-run gains are even greater.

Second, tax analysis usually ignores risk. Such neglect can become a major problem because the current income tax discriminates against risky equity investment in favor of safe debt investments. Such discrimination appears to violate principles of optimal taxation: if both risky and safe assets produce income for future consumption, why should the tax system discriminate between alternative investment strategies? Consumption taxation would eliminate this discrimination and would thereby improve both the allocation of capital and the incentives to save. Even some partial reforms would have substantial value. This study shows that eliminating the debt-equity distinction in the tax code may by itself achieve half the benefits of moving completely to a consumption tax.

Third, tax analyses usually focus on the labor supply and the formation of physical capital. Because human capital is more important than physical capital in a modern economy, the limitation is serious. Many economists argue that the current tax and education systems put little tax burden on the formation of human capital; that position would seem to justify the focus on the taxation of physical capital. This chapter makes two points. First, adding the formation of human capital to the analysis increases the estimated benefits from tax reform even if the incentives for investment in human capital are undistorted. Second, the study argues against the conventional view by pointing to the large amount of educational expenditures, both private and public, that most proposals for tax reform would include in the tax base. The inclusion violates the principle of a consumption tax because a true consumption tax would define the tax base as output minus all investment expenditures.

These three considerations—imperfect competition, risk, and the accumulation of human capital—all indicate that consumption taxation is even more beneficial, both in the long run and during transition, than generally argued. Such presentations initially ignore the impact of distribution. Two important points relate to concerns about distribution. First, some analyses argue that the elderly may lose from tax reform. A switch to consumption taxation may cause them to pay new taxes on their wealth either directly or implicitly through a decline in asset values. In particular, Gravelle (1995) predicts a

20–30 percent fall in stock prices if the Hall-Rabushka flat tax is passed. Such arguments typically assume perfect competition, whereby no firms earn any economic rents. Although farms and other small businesses may be competitive, they are not part of anybody's stock portfolio. It is difficult to view firms such as Microsoft, GM, and Boeing as perfectly competitive price takers. Their CEOs would not last long in their jobs if they were satisfied with normal profits and did not pursue opportunities to earn extranormal profits for their shareholders. Thus, this study argues that any predictions of collapses in asset prices are blunted, possibly even reversed, when an analysis includes imperfect competition. The presence of imperfect competition implies that firms earn pure profits on extra production and that the increase in future output induced by the flat tax (or any other consumption tax) would cause asset prices to rise immediately. The increase in asset prices would allow elderly asset holders to participate at once in the future benefits of tax reform and would make tax reform more uniformly beneficial across the generations.

Second, many middle-class families would lose from tax reform because of the loss of deductions for home mortgage interest and for state and local taxes. Some economists propose keeping the deduction for mortgage interest to avoid middle-class losses and to get that group to join the political coalition for a consumption tax. But retention of those deductions would substantially reduce the potential gains in efficiency from tax reform because the current bias against nonresidential business investment would continue. An alternative adjustment in tax reform proposals would allow the deductibility of some educational expenditures. The deduction would mitigate the issue of distribution since the adjustment could be aimed at middle-class taxpayers but would not deviate from the principle of a consumption tax.

Many proposals for a consumption tax have been put forward, including those described in Bradford 1986, Hall and Rabushka 1983, McLure and Zodrow 1996, and Weidenbaum 1996. Consumption tax principles also apply to any proposal for a value-added tax (VAT) or a national sales tax (NST) because either would eliminate the taxation of income on new investment. This analysis does not focus on any one proposal since the arguments for consumption taxation made here apply to all of them. Other proposals argue for eliminating the double taxation of equity income through the integration of individual and corporate taxation, thereby eliminating the asymmetric treatment of equity and debt assets (see Treasury 1992). Many of the results here also apply to those proposals because the focus is on the taxation of capital income. Similarly, the arguments in this chapter apply to features of more conventional tinkering with the tax code, such as the reintroduction of the investment tax credit. The results here show the importance of including imperfect competition, risk, and the formation of human capital to the analysis of any tax reform proposal.

The case for consumption taxation is strong and is even strengthened by including those features that make our economy a modern and technologically advanced one. Recognition of those elements should help us achieve substantive tax reform.

Evaluating Alternative Tax Systems

This section presents the conceptual foundation for this study. Any tax system produces distortions and damages economic performance. The task of policymakers is to choose a tax policy that inflicts the least damaging pattern of distortions. The task is particularly difficult in a dynamic economy, where one needs to trade off distortions today against their future consequences.

The arguments in this chapter rely on two basic results from optimal tax theory plus an argument from monopolistic competition theory. First, the inverse elasticity rule argues that the tax on a good should be inversely proportional to its demand and supply elasticities.[3] This study shows how to apply that rule to dynamic contexts and why an income tax is really a particularly ineffective kind of consumption tax.

Second, the Diamond and Mirrlees principle of productive efficiency argues against the taxation of intermediate goods, such as capital. The current tax system discriminates in favor of capital in the form of owner-occupied housing and against capital used to produce other goods. The system also treats human capital and physical capital differently even though both are essentially intermediate goods. Financial structure is also a type of intermediate good because debt and equity have no direct consumption value, but the current tax system discriminates against equity and in favor of debt. The principle of productive efficiency helps us understand what a true consumption tax would look like and why deviations from the principle of productive efficiency are so damaging to economic efficiency.

Third, this study displays similarities between taxation and imperfect competition. Any firm with some control over the price that it charges for its goods will charge a price in excess of marginal cost. That gap is similar to a tax. Recognizing the presence of imperfect competition is similar to recognizing the presence of other taxing authorities. The presence of these other "taxes" significantly affects our view of the government's taxes.

Inverse Elasticity Rule and Taxation of Asset Income. The inverse elasticity rule says that the optimal tax on a commodity is inversely proportional to its demand elasticity.[4] The two demand curves displayed in figure 2–1 illustrate this. Both goods are assumed to have a constant unit marginal cost. The demand curve for good 1 in the left half of figure 2–1 displays the impact of a tax equal to τ_1. The box R_1 is the revenue raised by the tax, CS_1, the consumer surplus, and H_1, the efficiency cost of the tax. Demand for good 2, displayed in the right half of figure 2–1, is assumed to be less elastic. If we imposed the same tax rate of τ_1 on good 2, the revenue is R_2, and the welfare cost is H_2. Because the demand for good 2 is less elastic, the optimal policy is to tax good 2 at a higher rate, say τ_2. The higher tax increases revenue by

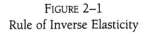

FIGURE 2–1
Rule of Inverse Elasticity

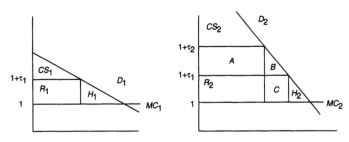

an amount equal to the area in box A minus the area in box C. The extra efficiency cost is $B + C$. The objective is to equate the marginal cost of a higher tax per dollar of revenue across different goods. That is accomplished by imposing higher taxes on the less elastically demanded goods. In figure 2–1 we would set the tax on good 1 at τ_1 and choose a higher tax of τ_2 on good 2.

Although the inverse elasticity rule may not seem to apply to discussions of income taxation and savings, it is the best way to view income taxation. Suppose that the different goods in figure 2–1 represent the consumption of goods and leisure at different dates. Income taxation implies a pattern of distortion across consumption and leisure at various dates. For example, if we save some money at time 0 for consumption at time t, then a tax on investment income essentially taxes consumption at time t. Suppose that r is the before-tax interest rate and t is the tax rate on interest. The social cost of one unit of consumption at time t in units of the time 0 good is $(1 + r)^{-t}$ and the after-tax price is $(1 + (1 - \tau)r)^{-t}$. This implies a tax distortion between MRS, the marginal rate of substitution between time t consumption and time 0 consumption, and MRT, the corresponding marginal rate of transformation, equal to

$$\frac{MRS}{MRT} = \left(\frac{1 + r}{1 + (1 - \tau)r} \right)^t . \tag{2–1}$$

This distortion is the same as if we taxed consumption at time t at the rate

$$\tau_c^* = \left(\frac{1 + r}{1 + (1 - \tau)r} \right)^t - 1. \tag{2–2}$$

Most important, the commodity tax equivalent here is exploding exponentially in time.

The situation is displayed in figure 2–2 with the demand for the time t consumption good relative to some untaxed good c_0 (such as time 0 leisure). This

FIGURE 2-2

Commodity Tax Equivalents of Taxation of Asset Income

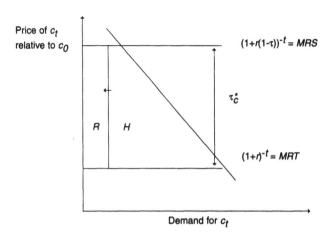

income tax is equivalent to a commodity tax on time t consumption equal to τ_c^* per unit of the time t good. We make the common assumption that the consumption demand curves are identical and independent across time and are not affected by leisure. The optimal tax system would impose the same tax on consumption at each different time. Instead, a constant positive interest tax is equivalent to an exponentially growing tax on time t consumption and thereby strongly violates the rule of inverse elasticity. In figure 2–2, as t increases, the deadweight loss triangle, H, grows more rapidly than the revenue box, R.

The exponential explosion in equation 2–2 appears dramatic, but we need to check that it is quantitatively important over a reasonable horizon. Table 2–1 displays the consumption tax equivalents, τ_c^*, for various combinations of r and τ. The results depend substantially on the magnitude of r. For $r = .01$, the mean real return on safe assets, the effects are small. For example, even a 50 percent tax on interest income implies only a 22 percent tax on consumption in forty years, compared with a 0.1 percent tax on consumption a year away. However, the situation is much different when $r = .10$. When $\tau = .3$ (which is less than the tax rate on equity-financed capital), the effective consumption tax over a one-year horizon is 3 percent, but it is 59 percent over a ten-year horizon and a whopping 543 percent over a forty-year horizon. It is hard to imagine any government passing a 59 percent sales tax in 2008, but that is effectively what we do to many investors if we continue with an income tax system into 2008.

The implications of this analysis are clear. If utility is separable across time and between consumption and leisure, and if the elasticity of demand for consumption does not change over time, the best tax system would have an

TABLE 2–1
Consumption Tax Equivalents, τ^*_c

		t					
r	τ	1	5	10	20	30	40
.01	10	0.1	.5	1	2	3	4
	30	0.3	1	3	6	9	13
	50	0.5	2	5	20	16	22
.10	10	1	5	10	20	31	44
	30	3	15	32	74	129	202
	50	5	26	59	154	304	543

equivalent of a constant commodity tax. A constant tax on consumption could accomplish that. However, any nonzero tax on asset income produces substantial violations.

While the exposition above focuses on special cases, the result is robust. Judd (1985b, 1999) shows that the optimal tax on asset income is zero in the long run, even when preferences are far more general than those used in dynamic tax analyses. Most important, exploding tax rates on consumption are not efficient, and the explosion is quantitatively important.

The result does not assume that everyone is the same. The result holds for each individual if his tastes do not change significantly over time. Therefore, even if tastes vary across individuals, each individual will prefer a constant consumption tax to an income tax that extracts the same revenue from him.

The inverse elasticity rule argues for a different tax on all goods, whereas proposals for a consumption tax actually prefer a single tax rate. While the difference may appear to be a serious difficulty, we will ignore it here. This approach is supported by the arguments of Balcer and his colleagues (1983). They show that while an optimal commodity tax system would have very different rates across goods, a revenue-equivalent flat tax is almost as good. Given the extra complexity and administrative cost of a tax system that charges different tax rates on different goods, a uniform consumption tax seems sensible.

The analysis does not necessarily imply that there should be no taxation of asset income. Suppose that tastes depend on age. If we assume that the elasticity of demand for consumption fell with age in just the right way, then a constant interest rate tax would be optimal; this result would require the demand curve in figure 2–2 for the time t good to become less elastic as t increases. Such an age-dependence could result with just the right interaction between consumption demand and leisure. However, advocates of taxing asset income apparently do not use this approach.[5] Such arguments must be fragile; our knowledge of the critical elasticities is too imprecise for such a purpose. In any case, it is hard to imagine demand elasticities changing enough to justify substantial taxation of asset income. In particular, table 2–1 tells us that to justify a 30 percent income tax if $r = 0.1$ over a twenty-year horizon, we would need consumption elasticity to fall by a factor of 25 over those twenty years—a rather implausible situation. Therefore, the case of constant elasticity is a reasonable one to use.

The distinction between the taxation of factor income and the taxation of commodities is misleading because none of the problems in figure 2–2 apply to taxation of wage income. If τ_L is a constant tax on wages and τ_K a constant rate tax on interest income, the MRS/MRT distortion between time 0 consumption and time t leisure is

$$\left(\frac{MRS}{MRT}\right)_{c_0, l_t} = \left(\frac{1}{1 - \tau_L}\right)\left(\frac{1 + r}{1 + (1 - \tau_K)r}\right)^t. \qquad (2\text{--}3)$$

Equation 2–3 represents how taxes distort decisions to sacrifice consumption at time 0 to gain extra leisure at time t. The distortion grows over time but only because of the interest income tax. The taxation of wages does not aggravate the distortions in savings, but taxation of asset income does aggravate distortions between consumption and leisure at different dates.

Commodity taxation and the inverse elasticity rule reveal many features of factor taxation. That view shows us how distortionary the taxation of asset income is and hints at the value of removing it from tax systems.

Productive Efficiency. The second important principle is the Diamond-Mirrlees result about productive efficiency. The essential argument is that a tax system may unavoidably cause distortions in consumption, but there is no need to force the economy to produce that output in an inefficient fashion. Primarily, the Diamond-Mirrlees result implies that an optimal tax system would tax only final goods, not intermediate goods.

For example, we may want to tax clothing and meat, but we do not want to tax sewing machines and meat storage lockers. If we taxed sewing machines, clothing producers would substitute away from mechanical production and toward labor-intensive methods and would thereby reduce the productivity of the economy. Even if we wanted to tax clothing more heavily than meat, any differential treatment of sewing machines and meat storage lockers would merely distort the allocation of capital. In any case, consumers would ultimately pay the taxes on sewing machines and meat lockers. Direct taxation of clothing and meat consumption would allow the production of both to proceed undistorted by the taxation of capital inputs.

The principle of productive efficiency applies to any analysis of income taxation, as capital goods are intermediate goods. In fact, the taxation of capital goods is equivalent to sales taxation of intermediate goods. For example, a 100 percent sales tax on capital equipment is equivalent to a 50 percent tax on the income flow from that capital equipment. Because the taxation of intermediate goods would generally reduce the productivity of an economy, the taxation of capital income would likely produce similar factor distortions, particularly if there were many capital goods.

Combining the principle of productive efficiency with the principle of inverse elasticity produces a strong case against the taxation of capital income. The differential taxation of capital goods would produce inefficiencies in the allocation of productive inputs. A uniform tax on capital inputs might not distort allocation but would effectively create an exploding consumption tax, as illustrated in table 2–1. Therefore, an optimal tax structure would tax only final goods.

Arguments for tax reform recognize the principle of productive efficiency. One of the key benefits from consumption taxation is the elimination of differential taxation across various capital goods (see Auerbach 1989 and Goulder and Thalmann 1993 for recent examinations of the importance of productive efficiency). The changes in 1986 attempted to create uniform taxation across capital goods. Auerbach (1989) argues that any optimal deviations are small under perfect competition.

Because the Diamond-Mirrlees principle does rely on special assumptions, some argue against its relevance in tax discussions. Two provisos immediately come to mind. First, Diamond and Mirrlees assume that each commodity is taxed at a separate rate. Again, as above, that is not a serious problem. Although Balcer and his colleagues (1983) did not consider a general equilibrium case where intermediate goods could be taxed, their conclusion—that uniform taxation is almost as good as the optimal nonuniform tax—seems robust. Second, the result from productive efficiency also assumes that all pure profits are taxed away, whereas pure profits are not taxed away in the current tax system or in any proposed reform. In fact, the drop in marginal rates from most reforms would reduce the taxation of pure rents. This chapter shows that the result is not a serious impediment to applying the production efficiency principle when we use estimates for tastes and technology.

The Diamond-Mirrlees principle of productive efficiency provides a theoretical basis for consumption taxation. However, the principle also tells us that we need to pay careful attention to what is an intermediate good and what is a final good. The distinction plays a critical role in the following discussion of human capital.

Imperfect Competition and Taxation. The third idea used in this study is that government decisions about taxation and the distortions produced by imperfect competition in the private sector have similar implications. A firm that charges a price above marginal cost is effectively acting as a tax collector.

FIGURE 2–3
Taxation and Monopolistic Competition

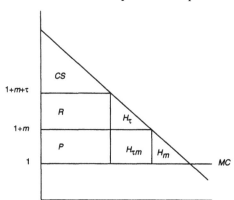

Any national consumption or income tax is imposed on top of any distortions in the private sector. The accumulation of distortions substantially affects estimates of the burden of taxes and the relative evaluation of consumption and income tax systems.

The key principles are displayed in figure 2–3. Suppose that a good is not sold at its marginal cost, equal to 1 in figure 2–3, but is sold at a marked-up price, $1 + m$. The markup can arise and be sustained for many reasons. The producer may have market power because of large fixed costs of entry or because his product is differentiated from the products of competitors. Alternatively, the producer may hold a patent, which makes him a legal monopolist.

Any markup above marginal cost acts essentially as a tax. In figure 2–3, H_m is the efficiency cost of such a markup, just as H_1 and H_2 were the efficiency costs of taxation in figure 2–1. The box $P + H_{\tau m}$ is the monopolists' "tax revenue," consisting of profits in excess of economic costs. The economic effect of any markup is similar to that of taxation since both cause the buyer to pay a price in excess of the true marginal cost. These two cases differ in who receives the markup: the government in the case of a tax and a private firm in the case of a markup. Both taxation and markups create efficiency losses and rents.

This work relies heavily on the analogy between taxation by the government and markups arising from imperfect competition. The analogy is particularly appropriate in the case of patents. The holder of a patent is not necessarily a monopoly producer. In fact, many patent holders do not produce their product. The key feature of a patent is that the patent holder can impose a tax on the purchase of the patented good, either directly through producing the good and charging a price in excess of marginal cost or indirectly through a royalty. Those distortions reduce economic efficiency and lead to underproduction of the patented good, but are justified by the incentives that they create for innovation. Without the rents produced by a patent, an innovator would not have sufficient incentive to undertake the fixed costs of research and development; that situation could lead to an even worse condition of no production of a desirable product. Therefore, even though patent monopolies reduce efficiency just as taxes do, we would not want to destroy the rents that they create.

The story of the patent monopoly is the simplest one to illustrate the key arguments, but the arguments are robust and apply to any context in which firms charge a price in excess of marginal cost. In many cases, these markups occur because of product differentiation and increasing returns to scale, conditions that share many features of a patent monopoly even without a formal property right. This study revolves around the presence of a markup of price over marginal cost, whether it arises from patent monopoly, an oligopoly of differentiated competitors, or another form of imperfect competition.

Markups may also occur because of collusion or corruption, but those matters are the concern and responsibility of antitrust policy. The arguments here apply to imperfect competition that remains after appropriate application of antitrust laws. I do not argue that tax policy is a substitute for antitrust policy. Instead, I argue that tax policy should take notice that imperfect competition is an important part of any modern economy.

Suppose that we introduce a tax τ into an imperfectly competitive market. The buyer now pays both the markup and the tax, resulting in a total price of $1 + m + \tau$. The $m + \tau$ portion acts as a tax, raising the price above the marginal cost and producing revenues now for the government. In this case, the government's revenue is the box R, and the firm's profits are P. The tax τ causes the monopolist to lose profits and causes the consumers to lose H_τ in consumer surplus. The cost of the tax is not just a triangle of consumer surplus but also a box $H_{\tau m}$ of pure profits. The efficiency cost of the tax is now larger relative to the revenue raised because of the preexisting distortion.

Joan Robinson (1934) noticed those facts and argued that a good tax policy would use subsidies to bring buyer price down to a social marginal cost. That argument would imply that in figure 2–3 we would want to pay the buyer a subsidy equal to the markup m. Robinson also argued that the policy would have some undesirable effects because it would increase monopoly profits and would likely be regressive in its impact on income distribution. Because taxing away those extra profits would be difficult, she did not endorse such an approach.

We argue that these distributional concerns are not important in the U.S. economy. In modern dynamic economies, a firm has difficulty in maintaining large monopoly rents. High profits encourage entry by imitators. We thought of IBM as a firm with large market power before it was hit by competition from producers of personal computers and workstations. For many firms, the current profits arising from setting prices above marginal costs are necessary to recover R&D costs and other fixed costs of production. Hall (1986) supports such a view of monopolistic competition; he finds scant evidence of supernormal returns to firms even though he finds that prices substantially exceed marginal costs.

This study makes limited use of the ideas of imperfect competition. The key idea is that preexisting distortions increase the efficiency cost of government taxation, even if tax policy is not used to fine-tune those distortions. We see below how this limited argument strengthens the case for consumption taxation.

Taxation in a Simple Dynamic Competitive Model. Some standard analyses can illustrate the significant benefits of moving away from the taxation of income asset and toward the taxation of consumption. We assume the simple growth model in Judd 1987. Most important, output is produced by capital and labor and is divided into consumption and investment. There are no adjustment costs. We use the representative agent paradigm. We assume a Cobb-Douglas production function with capital share of .25. We also assume that the labor supply has a compensated elasticity[6] equal to $\eta > 0$, that the consumption demand elasticity is $\gamma > 0$, and that tastes are separable between consumption and leisure. We assume a proportional tax on labor income at a rate of τ_L and a proportional tax on capital income at rate τ_K.

Table 2–2 displays the marginal efficiency cost of various tax changes for values of γ and η. We assume that the economy begins with one tax policy and makes minor changes in the taxation of labor or capital income or introduces a small investment tax credit (ITC) applied to all investment. We do not explicitly include a consumption tax, but an increase in an ITC has the same effect of reducing the effective tax on new capital without reducing the taxation of old capital. For example, the flat tax proposes the expensing of capital expenditures, a measure equivalent to a large ITC. The three policy tools cover most policy options used in the past and proposed for the future.

We first examine the case where $\tau_L = \tau_K = .3$ initially, and then we examine the case where the economy begins with $\tau_L = .4$ and $\tau_K = .5$. MEB_L is the marginal loss of utility (measured in dollars) per dollar of revenue raised if τ_L is increased. MEB_K (MEB_{ITC}) is the corresponding index for increases in τ_K (an ITC). The MEB indexes in table 2–2 are discounted present values that include the transition process from one tax policy regime to another. We expect the $MEB > 0$ because we expect that any change in tax policy that raises revenues will reduce utility; however, $MEB < 0$ is possible in severely distorted systems.

Table 2–2 illustrates several important points. First, we do not have an adequate quantitative grasp of the welfare costs of tax changes. The values of critical parameters used in table 2–2 are all in the range of existing empirical estimates. Choosing among the empirical estimates of γ and η is difficult because they have different data sets and estimation strategies. The typical approach to calibration would vigorously argue for one particular parameter choice and would ignore others. I am skeptical about our ability to make such

TABLE 2-2

Efficiency Costs of Various Policy Changes

γ	η	$\tau_L = .3, \tau_K = .3$			$\tau_L = .4, \tau_K = .5$		
		MEB_L	MEB_K	MEB_{ITC}	MEB_L	MEB_K	MEB_{ITC}
.1	.1	.02	.15	.46	.04	.38	1.1
.1	.4	.04	.21	.72	.07	.51	1.8
.1	1.0	.05	.25	.99	.08	.62	2.5
.5	.1	.04	.36	1.9	.07	1.3	-15
.5	.4	.11	.42	2.6	.21	1.5	-9.8
.5	1.0	.19	.48	4.0	.35	1.7	-7.3
2.0	.1	.05	.69	-240.0	.09	5.8	-2.8
2.0	.4	.20	.91	-6.9	.39	22.	-2.4
2.0	1.0	.50	1.3	-3.5	1.19	-11.	-2.0

choices, given the noisy data available and the enormous gap between any model and the far more complex real world.

Second, table 2-2 shows that we do not need good estimates to rank alternative changes in tax policy. In all cases in table 2-2, replacing the taxation of capital income with the taxation of labor income would improve welfare, usually by a substantial amount relative to the revenue shift. Furthermore, changes that focus on encouraging new investment, such as an ITC, are particularly effective in improving economic performance with only a slight loss in revenue. In fact, MEB_{ITC} is sometimes negative; in such cases, an increase in an ITC would raise revenues because the extra revenue from the tax on new capital and the extra taxation from the higher wages would pay for the costs of the investment tax credit. An increase in an ITC is similar to the introduction of a flat tax. Both would reduce the taxation of new investment but would not reduce the tax burden on old capital. Indeed, the flat tax can be viewed as an income tax at rate τ plus an ITC at rate τ without depreciation allowances.

Third, the more elastic the labor supply is, the greater the difference between MEB_L and MEB_K. A static perspective suggests that the relative costs of the taxation of labor and of capital income depend on the elasticities of savings and the labor supply and that as the elasticity of the labor supply increased, the welfare cost of the taxation of labor relative to the taxation of capital income would rise. The opposite is true in table 2-2, where both MEB_K and MEB_{ITC} rise even more rapidly than MEB_L as we increase the elasticity of the labor supply, η. The resolution of the puzzle lies in the MRS/MRT distortion expressions, equations 2–1 and 2–3. According to those equations, the taxation of asset income implies an exploding distortion for both consumption and leisure demand. As the elasticity of the labor supply rises, the importance of this distortion in the labor market also rises because the taxation of asset income rises.

The case of $\tau_L = \tau_K = .3$ for the initial tax policy is less taxing than current tax rates. The case of $\tau_L = .4$ and $\tau_K = .5$ is closer to the conventional description of the tax system before 1981, but it is not generally considered descriptive of the current tax system. Of course, the welfare benefits of tax reduction are much greater when we begin with higher tax rates. We also see that the scenario of $\tau_L = .4$ and $\tau_K = .5$ is actually plausible with the impact of imperfect competition.

The robustness of the results in table 2–2 is surprising because we normally expect results from computational general equilibrium to depend critically on the elasticity parameters. The magnitudes of the *MEB* indexes do depend on elasticity values, but the ranking of alternative policies does not. Some fundamental principle is present here. We argue that the critical facts come from optimal tax theory: the taxation of asset income corresponds to exploding commodity taxation, but the taxation of labor and the taxation of consumption do not.

Optimal Tax Theory and Tax Reform. Before continuing, it is important to summarize the theoretical arguments used here because the results strongly contradict the standard intuition used by many analysts in the tax reform literature.

Gravelle's (1994) comparison of the welfare effects of consumption taxation and of capital income taxation is a good statement of the commonsense approach. She asserts that

> theory does not tell us, a priori, whether eliminating capital income taxes will increase overall efficiency, since it reduces one distortion at the price of increasing another . . . . The efficiency effects depend on assumptions about behavioral effects. If individuals are relatively unwilling to substitute consumption over time and relatively willing to substitute leisure for consumption of goods, then a significant tax on capital income would constitute part of an optimal tax system. These behavioral effects are difficult to estimate empirically. (p. 31)

This intuition is a natural one. Its references to substitution propensities appear to invoke the inverse elasticity rule, also invoked here, and argue that we must accept trade-offs among various distortions. However, the arguments of this chapter do not make any qualifications concerning the relative elasticity of intertemporal substitution and the labor supply. Some earlier analyses made assumptions of separability, but even those assumptions are absent in

Judd 1985b. Many analyses arguing against long-run taxation of capital assume a constant intertemporal elasticity of consumption, but that focus is not restrictive. Table 2–1 shows that even a small tax on capital income implies rapidly exploding consumption tax equivalents, and there is no evidence that individual consumption elasticities vary enough to make such a tax policy efficient. Plausible values for elasticities in consumption demand and in the labor supply offer no support for the taxation of asset income in the long run.

This discussion ignores the transition process, but there again we find no evidence supporting the taxation of asset income on the basis of efficiency. Table 2–2 shows the opposite. The gaps MEB_{ITC} - MEB_L and MEB_K - MEB_L represent the efficiency gain from increasing the taxation on *labor* and using the revenues to finance an increase in the ITC or a decrease in the taxation of capital income. Table 2–2 shows that the gain increases as we increase our estimate of the elasticity of the labor supply. As the elasticity of the labor supply increases, it is more valuable to increase the taxation of *labor* income and to reduce the taxation of *capital* income, even when we consider the process of transition.

The theoretical case against the taxation of capital income in favor of the taxation of consumption is much stronger than conventionally thought. There are qualifiers, of course. Hubbard and Judd (1986, 1988) show that the taxation of asset income may be desirable when capital markets are imperfect. The intuition there is straightforward: the taxation of capital income may be useful if it is a substitute for missing capital markets. However, those findings are sensitive to the nature of market incompleteness. It is unclear if those considerations can justify observed tax rates on capital income. For example, it is difficult to imagine that liquidity constraints could justify the corporate income tax. Capital market failures might be better resolved through more modest adjustments of a consumption tax.

We have so far considered the choice between consumption and income taxation in the simplest possible model: perfect capital markets, perfect competition, no risk, and only physical capital and raw labor inputs. We now deviate from this simple model and show that the case for consumption taxation is strengthened.

Imperfect Competition and the Benefits of Consumption Taxation

Tax reform analyses usually assume perfect competition in all markets. But that condition is not a valid description of a modern economy. Although no one would disagree with that assertion, the implications for tax policy are not immediately clear. This chapter argues that the presence of imperfect competition strengthens the case for consumption taxation.

Basically, let us pursue an intuitive combination of two well-known ideas.

First is the Robinson argument that subsidies can be used to offset the distortions if a lump-sum tax is available. At first, that position seems to have limited usefulness because it would imply that most goods would be subsidized—what would be left to tax to finance these subsidies as well as normal expenditures? Second, Diamond and Mirrlees (1971) tell us that only final goods should be taxed, not intermediate goods. Since markups are similar to taxation, then the final net tax on intermediate goods should be zero, no matter what the impact on the taxation of final goods. In combination, these principles indicate that final goods should be taxed to finance corrective subsidies of any intermediate goods, including capital goods, sold at a price above marginal cost.

This study makes only a limited use of that controversial assertion. The pure theoretical argument ignores many practical difficulties, and it would be impractical to construct the perfect corrective policy. Our theory still has practical consequences: if reducing price-cost margins for intermediate goods were optimal, then imposing taxes that aggravated price-cost margins for intermediate goods could not be a sensible idea. In a competitive world, a low tax on intermediate goods may cause only minimal damage to the economy's efficiency. In a world with imperfect competition in intermediate-goods industries, even a low tax on intermediate goods could cause substantial damage.

Because taxes on asset income are equivalent to taxes on intermediate goods, low taxes on asset income can create major losses in efficiency. That possibility strengthens the case for switching away from tax systems, such as the conventional taxation on income, that aggravate the distortions of imperfect competition, and toward consumption tax policies.

Financing Social Fixed Costs and Taxation. The results here may at first appear strange and in conflict with the principles of free-market economics. Before giving a more concrete analysis, this chapter presents a simple example of fixed costs in production, with the application of the Diamond-Mirrlees model and a comparison of its prescriptions with the actual financing of fixed costs.

Suppose that one capital good, call it computers, has a constant unit cost after some large fixed cost is paid for, say, R&D. That good cannot be produced in a perfectly competitive market because a price equal to marginal cost will not allow the firm to recover the initial fixed costs. Some deviation from competitive pricing must finance this fixed cost. The Diamond-Mirrlees principle says that the optimal way to finance the fixed cost for computers is to tax final goods only. The pattern of the taxation of final goods is governed by the inverse elasticity rule, not by the goods using computers in their manufacture.

Compare that example with how we actually finance fixed costs, such as R&D expenditures. The computer manufacturer needs to limit competition so that it can charge a markup over marginal cost sufficient to finance the fixed cost. The economies of scale may be sufficient to deter entry, or perhaps the computer manufacturer can get a patent on computers. How market power is attained is not particularly important, but some form of market power is necessary.

The need to deviate from perfect competition to create the proper incentives for innovation has long been recognized. The U.S. Constitution specifically recognizes the need "to promote the progress of science and useful arts, by securing for limited times to authors and inventors the exclusive right to their respective writings and discoveries." Patents and copyrights create market power and are valuable instruments to encourage innovation. Because innovation is an important policy concern of government, it is natural for tax policy to be designed to avoid any interference with innovation policy.

The analysis here has avoided any explicit modeling of innovation. Innovation in a dynamic world has been modeled in many ways (see Judd 1985a for an example and Barro and Sala-I-Martin 1995 for a review of the literature). For the sake of simplicity, this chapter assumes that tax policy has no impact on innovation. If endogenous innovation were included, then moving to a consumption tax would increase innovation in capital goods and would further increase the estimates of the gains from consumption tax reform. The differences would be sensitive to details that are difficult to estimate. This chapter takes a more conservative approach with the sole focus on the distortions of imperfect competition and the price-cost margins, which are easier to estimate.

The incidence of market power in a patent or similar system of protection for intellectual property would probably differ greatly from the incidence of the distortions in the ideal Diamond-Mirrlees scheme. Only computer users would pay the markup in computers. Those users would substitute away from computers and toward alternative intermediate goods. The markup in computer prices would most affect those final goods that used computers in their production. An inefficient pattern of distortions across final goods would result because those computer-intensive products might not be the ones taxed in an optimal Diamond-Mirrlees scheme. The impossibility of attaining the perfect Diamond-Mirrlees set of distortions only strengthens the case here because the excessive burden imposed by imperfect competition on intermediate goods would only be further aggravated by any taxation of capital income.

Economic growth requires the creation of some incentives for innovation. The patent and copyright systems succeed in that, but they create distortions in the private sectors. Therefore, tax policy in a modern economy operates in a world already distorted by other "taxes." We will see that this insight has important consequences for the value of consumption taxation.

Empirical Evidence on Imperfect Competition. Let us examine the evidence that there is significant imperfect competition. Many studies have considered the gap between prices and marginal costs. Furthermore, the empirical literature on industrial organization contains some industry-specific studies on price-cost margins. The studies also estimate price-cost margins in the 20 percent range for some capital goods (see, for example, Appelbaum 1982). Both Hall (1986) and Domowitz, Hubbard, and Petersen (1988) indicate that the margins in the equipment sectors are substantial, generally 15– 40 percent of the price. There is little reason to doubt the presence of significant economies of scale and significant deviations of price over marginal cost. Even a lower estimate of 10 percent is sizable: it is equivalent to a 10 percent sales tax on such equipment.

Fortunately, the discussion here does not rely critically on these estimates of price-cost margins, especially for investment goods. In particular, R&D expenditures in 1990 equaled 9.2 percent of sales for machinery and 4.7 percent for electrical equipment. Learning curves also produce increasing returns to scale that act essentially as a fixed initial cost. Those considerations plus a conservative estimate of economies of scale and other long-run fixed costs put us in a range relevant for these policy discussions. Therefore, even under conservative readings of the empirical evidence, the importance of imperfect competition appears substantial.

A Simple Model of Imperfect Competition. A simple dynamic model examined in Judd 1997 formally establishes the argument here. It makes a few key assumptions. First, the number of goods, all produced in a monopolistically competitive market, is fixed. Thus, marginal increases in demand result in pure profits for all firms. Each good can be used for both consumption and investment, and each good is used in the production of all goods. The representative agent model in Judd 1997 also assumes an elastic labor supply.

We assume that pure profits are taxed at the rate τ_{π} and that income on marginal physical investment is taxed at rate τ_D. One interpretation is that the equity holders of each firm own a patent on its good and use debt to finance any physical investment. In equilibrium, the return on equity is the pure rent associated with holding the patent, and debt holders receive the marginal product of the physical investment. Therefore, dividend income is subject to taxation at the corporate and individual levels, but the debt-financed physical capital income is taxed only at the personal level.

Cost of capital with imperfect competition in capital goods markets. We next illustrate how the social cost of capital is altered by a combination of income taxation and imperfect competition. The cost of capital is determined by the usual arbitrage condition. Suppose that a firm is contemplating buying one more unit of capital with a social marginal cost of production equal to 1. Because of the markup m charged by the producer of the capital good, the investing firm pays $1 + m$ for the unit of capital. Suppose that the marginal product of capital is MPK. Assume that the firm's bondholders pay a tax τ_D on the earnings from this investment and receive an after-tax return of $\bar{r}$ on alternative investments. Investment will continue until the after-tax return (we assume no depreciation) from a one-unit investment, $MPK (1 - \tau_D)$, equals the opportunity cost of the investment, $\bar{r} (1 + m)$. In equilibrium, the level of investment is determined by

TABLE 2–3
Effective Total Tax Rates

| | τ_D | | | |
m	.1	.2	.3	.5
.05	.14	.24	.33	.52
.10	.18	.27	.36	.54
.20	.25	.33	.42	.58
.30	.31	.38	.46	.62

$$MPK = \bar{r}\, \frac{1 + m}{1 - \tau_D}. \tag{2-4}$$

If $m = 0$, equation 2–4 is the usual cost of capital formula. In the presence of monopolistic competition, the upstream markup of m on the purchase of capital goods acts in the same way as the downstream taxation of interest income.

To illustrate the combined effects of taxation and imperfect competition, we derive an effective combined tax rate. The situation in equation 2–4 behaves as if there were no markup and as though the tax on interest income were equal to τ^* where

$$\tau^* = 1 - \frac{1 - \tau_D}{1 + m} = \tau_D + \frac{m}{1 + m}(1 - \tau_D). \tag{2-5}$$

Table 2–3 presents values for the total effective tax rate τ^* for various values of the explicit tax τ_D and the margin m. For low tax rates and margins, the total effective tax rate is the sum $\tau_D + m$. At greater rates, τ^* is less than $\tau_D + m$, but presence of the margin m still substantially increases the total distortion. For example, the presence of a 30 percent margin causes the total tax rate to be 38 percent if $\tau_D = .20$.

With the concept of effective total tax in equation 2–5, we can see how our earlier arguments apply. First, because markups on capital goods distort investment just as an interest tax would, they produce the same kind of exploding distortion in equation 2–2 that incurs under an interest tax. A uniform markup on capital goods violates the inverse elasticity principle just as a constant tax on asset income does.

Second, incorporating imperfect competition into our analysis forces us to reconsider the arguments regarding the level playing field. According to conventional wisdom, based on assumptions of perfect competition, the 1986 tax changes eliminated most of the differential taxation of capital goods; Auerbach 1989 is an example of such a study. Even if the explicit income taxes do not discriminate among alternative capital goods, the total effective tax rate τ^* will vary across goods to the extent that their margins vary. Studies such as Hall 1986 and Domowitz, Hubbard, and Petersen 1986 indicate substantial variance in margins among capital goods. Because the welfare costs of taxation are increasing in the variance of inappropriate distortions, our neglect of heterogeneous markups makes our results conservative estimates of the inefficiency associated with the taxation of capital income.

Optimal tax policy. This section illustrates what the presence of imperfect competition implies for optimal tax policy. We assume in this exercise that one can determine the markups and use them for policy purposes—although this is not a realistic assumption because of the difficulty in measuring markups with great precision. The purpose of this exercise is to illustrate how much the presence of markups could affect the optimal policy. The results strongly indicate how important imperfect competition is.

When pure profits are taxed at rate τ_π, Judd 1997 shows that the long-run optimal choice for τ_D is

$$\tau_D^{opt} = -m \; \frac{1 + \tau_\pi \; MEB}{1 + MEB} \qquad (2\text{--}6)$$

where m is the markup of price over marginal cost and MEB is again the marginal efficiency cost of taxation. If the efficiency cost of taxation is zero, then the optimal tax completely neutralizes the monopolistic price distortion. The result repeats the Robinson finding. As in Diamond-Mirrlees, the optimal tax rate on profits, τ_π, is 100 percent, and the optimal policy eliminates the monopolistic price distortion.

Although our optimal tax formula (equation 2–6) is simple, it is not immediately clear that the desirable subsidy is economically significant when we use reasonable values for the markup m, the profits tax τ_π, and the marginal excess burden, MEB. We assume $m \in [.1, .3]$, as suggested by our discussion of price-cost margins. The range for MEB is taken from table 2–2. A key fact is that the equilibrium in our monopolistic competition analysis is essentially the same as for the competitive model used in table 2–2 where τ^* from equation 2–5 is used as the total effective tax rate on capital income.

Table 2–4 shows that even if MEB is large, the optimal tax substantially reduces the monopolistic distortion. In that table we assume that $\tau_\pi = .2$, as proposed in the flat tax; we arrive at similar conclusions if we use the tax rate on pure profits implicit in any other major tax reform proposal.

Table 2–4 illustrates several points. First, the optimal subsidy is nontrivial in most cases. A system that puts no tax on asset income would still suffer a substantial distortion relative to the ideal. Second, the basic implications of optimal tax theory hold even though the profits tax is far less than desired by

TABLE 2–4
Optimal Tax Rates

m	MEB			
	.2	.5	1.0	2.0
.05	-.04	-.04	-.03	-.02
.10	-.09	-.07	-.06	-.05
.20	-.17	-.15	-.12	-.09
.30	-.26	-.22	-.18	-.14

Diamond-Mirrlees.[7] Third, the desire for productive efficiency is strong even when the marginal efficiency cost of taxation is high. The efficiency cost may be high because the revenue need is large or because the elasticity of the labor supply is high. In either case, tax policy should still focus on policies that do not aggravate the preexisting distortions from imperfect competition.

The policy implied by table 2–4 is impractical. However, the results indicate how far from optimal any income tax system is. The table also indicates how concerns about the taxation of pure profits are of far less importance than the goal of eliminating productive and intertemporal distortions.

Benefits of Switching to Consumption Taxation. Continuing with the model in Judd 1997, this section gives a quantitative estimate of how monopolistic competition affects the estimated gains from switching to a consumption tax. The estimated benefits of switching to a flat consumption tax are substantially increased with the presence of imperfect competition.

Because price-cost margins are essentially the same as taxes, we can use the results in table 2–2 to draw inferences about the benefits of minor changes in the tax policy. Suppose that capital goods are sold at 20 percent above marginal cost. We also assume that there are labor market imperfections, such as labor unions, that cause wage costs to be 10 percent higher. Then, even if the explicit taxes are $\tau_L = \tau_K = .3$ initially, the economy really begins with $\tau_L = .4$ and $\tau_K = .5$ when we change the tax policy. The $\tau_L = .4$, $\tau_K = .5$ case in table 2–2 then displays the efficiency impact of alternative tax changes if all marginal profits are taxed away. The marginal benefits of reducing taxation on asset income are substantially increased—being at least doubled and often at least tripled. The magnitudes are uncertain because the values of the critical taste parameters are unknown, but the impact of imperfect competition is clear and substantial for any standard estimate.

Table 2–2 examines marginal changes. We next examine major changes in tax policy. Table 2–5 presents the total welfare gain from replacing all income taxation with consumption taxation. Table 2–5 reports the percentage change

		τ_K		
γ	m	.15	.25	.35
.25	.0	.12	.38	.84
	.1	.37	.79	1.41
	.2	.54	1.08	1.81
.5	.0	.19	.59	1.30
	.1	.57	1.21	2.16
	.2	.81	1.62	2.74
1.1	.0	.24	.76	1.67
	.1	.72	1.54	2.75
	.2	1.00	2.04	3.46

TABLE 2–5
Welfare Gain
(percent of consumption)

in consumption equal to the change in welfare from the tax change. For example, when $\gamma = .25$, $m = 0$, and $\tau_K = .15$, the welfare gain from the switch is equal to an immediate and permanent .12 percent increase in consumption.[8] Table 2–5 examines tax rates of 15 percent, 25 percent, and 35 percent on capital income.[9] The rate τ_K represents the marginal tax rate, not the average rate, because the distortion depends on the marginal tax rate. We examine markups of 0 percent, 10 percent, and 20 percent. We assume depreciation at 5 percent per year and the capital share at 25 percent.

Table 2–5 shows that a markup substantially increases the benefits of switching to a consumption tax. In fact, just a 10 percent markup often doubles the welfare gain relative to the situation with perfect competition. Again, these gains are substantial for any estimate of the critical parameters.

Implications of Asset Pricing. There is substantial interest in the implications of tax reform on the pricing of assets. In particular, a move to a consumption tax would remove the tax burden on new capital but would continue taxing old capital. In a perfectly competitive world, where output depends on labor and physical capital alone, competition from new capital could lower the market value of old capital. Gravelle (1995) estimates that the Hall-Rabushka flat tax would cause a 20–30 percent fall in the stock market. If true, this important issue would create opposition to tax reform.

Gravelle's estimate assumes perfect competition. However, it is unrealistic to assume that most equity wealth is associated with perfectly competitive firms. The value of many firms consists not only of physical capital but also of intellectual capital. The value of computer software firms such as Microsoft and pharmaceutical firms such as Pfizer comes from their patents and copyrights, not from their physical plants. Patents and copyrights, as well as the costs of imitation, make competitive entry difficult. Although lower tax rates may spur new innovation, the R&D process takes time and has only delayed effects on the profits of incumbents.

Many firms are combinations of physical capital and intellectual capital. Tax reform would reduce the cost of physical capital to each firm and would thereby cause more competition among firms and lower prices. However, if a firm initially charged a price in excess of marginal cost, the increase in demand would increase profits. Predictions about asset prices need to be changed for an imperfectly competitive world. The tax analogy is again apt. Firms with market power essentially impose a tax on their customers. If the government reduced taxes on a firm's customers, then one would expect the firm to gain through increased demand for its product. For example, if the tax τ in figure 2–3 were eliminated, the firm's profits would increase by the box $H_{\tau m}$. The gain in profits would not exist for perfectly competitive producers and is ignored in analyses of changes in asset prices that assume perfect competition in the product markets.[10]

The intuition is clear and is similar to the situation of multiple tax jurisdictions. If the federal income tax were repealed and were replaced with lump-sum taxation, then output would rise, and revenues from state income taxes would rise. The same would be true when the producers imposed a tax on their customers; a more efficient U.S. tax system would increase the average firm's sales and would increase the revenue from the "tax" that it imposed on customers through the gap between price and marginal cost. For a private firm, these extra revenues, current and future, would immediately be capitalized in the firm's value.

Although the magnitude of those changes is not as clear, the impact in an open economy is: if interest rates do not change, then an increase in future profit flows will immediately increase asset values. However, a radical change in U.S. tax policy might produce changes in interest rates in our closed-economy model. We need to investigate that possibility to establish the robustness of our general claim that the impact of a consumption tax on asset prices is positively affected by the presence of imperfect competition.

We include that situation explicitly in the model in Judd 1997 with an inelastic labor supply. Essentially, we assume that all goods, final and intermediate, have a common markup, m. A reduction in the tax on capital income would cause an immediate increase in investment and a gradual increase in aggregate output. The share of output devoted to consumption and final goods would fluctuate, but that variation would not affect aggregate asset values because we assume that all goods have the same markup.[11]

Table 2–6 reports the initial impact on the aggregate market value of equity if we replace an income tax with a labor income tax in the model of Judd 1997. In such a tax system, the value of a firm would be equal to the replacement value of its assets if there were no adjustment costs (as we assume) and if product markets were perfectly competitive. We assume that the economy is initially in the steady state associated with a tax rate τ_K on all asset income. We also assume that fixed costs of production are so high that there are no extranormal profits in the initial steady state. We examine three cases for the intertemporal elasticity of substitution, γ; two values for the initial income tax rate, τ_K; and two possible values of the markup, m.

According to table 2–6, a transition to a labor tax or a lump-sum tax would result in an increase in asset values. The impact would be slight in the cases of small γ because of the slow adjustment in consumption and investment. The case of nearly log utility ($\gamma = 1.1$) and a modest markup of 20 percent implies that the value of a firm would rise by 13 percent if the marginal tax on equity capital were 35 percent. If a firm were financed half by debt and half by equity, all increased value would go to equity holders; the situation implies a 26 percent increase in the stock market value.

A flat tax would produce different results, but its implications are clear. If the flat tax rate were 20 percent, then the value of a perfectly competitive firm would fall by 20 percent because the expensing provisions would create a 20 percent wedge between the value of old and new capital. Gravelle (1995) makes this point. However, the change in the value of a noncompetitive firm would still be increased by the extra pure profits that it would earn. The net change would be equal to the value in table 2–6 minus 20 percent. Similar arguments apply to the case of a VAT or a national sales tax.

In all cases in table 2–6, imperfect competition reduces the negative impacts of consumption taxation on the welfare of those, like some elderly, who sell assets to finance consumption. Lyon and Merrill (chapter 3 in this volume) discuss the implications of asset prices in greater detail. They make similar points but do not consider equilibrium impacts on sales and interest rates. Their arguments further reduce any possible fall in asset prices. The simpler general equilibrium model used here explores the importance of imperfect competition and ignores many other elements considered by Lyon and Merrill. The arguments made here and in Lyon and Merrill reinforce each other and argue strongly against the pessimistic views in Gravelle 1995.

Imperfect Competition and Tax Reform. Imperfect competition is a fact in a modern economy and should be included in any tax analysis. Such competition provides incentives for innovation. Users of capital goods are already paying a tax to finance that investment. While relieving that tax burden may not be feasible through tinkering with the tax code, this private tax means that further taxation of capital goods would substantially damage economic efficiency. The private tax enhances the value of a move to consumption taxation.

TABLE 2–6
Initial Increase in Firm Value
from a Wage Tax
(in percent)

γ	m	τ_K		
		.15	.25	.35
.2	.1	1.1	2.0	3.1
	.2	1.8	3.3	5.2
	.3	2.3	4.4	6.8
.5	.1	1.8	3.3	5.4
	.2	3.0	5.7	9.3
	.3	4.1	7.8	12.9
1.1	.1	2.4	4.5	7.5
	.2	4.1	8.0	13.3
	.3	5.7	11.3	19.1

Imperfect competition also ameliorates any negative impact on asset prices because the increase in production increases pure profits. Including imperfect competition in this analysis improves the predictions for long-run growth, the benefits during transition, and the immediate impact on asset prices.

Risk and Tax Reform

Investment is generally risky, but tax reform analyses often ignore risk. This section uses Hamilton's (1987) general equilibrium analysis of the taxation of risky assets to make some basic points. First, the asymmetric treatment of risky assets will affect the equilibrium portfolio of the economy. Although expected, that finding emphasizes the importance of general equilibrium effects because partial equilibrium analyses lead to contrary conclusions. Second, Hamilton's finding that there should be no differential taxation of risky and safe assets indicates that a goal of tax reform should be the elimination of any distortion between safe and risky investments. Third, we analyze the utility-revenue trade-off available to policymakers and demonstrate the importance of incorporating risk in an analysis.

Asset Returns and Risk. The most important fact about asset returns in the United States is that the annual pretax real return to individuals on equity investments has averaged 7 percent with a standard deviation of 20 percent, and the mean real return on safe assets has been 1 percent. Corporate tax adjustments imply that both mean and variance should be 20–40 percent higher for the risky asset to approximate the opportunities offered to society. The extra return to risky equity is consistent with the standard theory of asset pricing, but the magnitude is difficult to explain (see Kocherlakota 1996 for a discussion of asset-pricing puzzles). The empirical puzzles surrounding asset pricing make any tax analysis difficult to execute. Even so, including risk in the analysis strengthens the case for consumption taxation.

Treatment of Risk in the U.S. Income Tax System. The U.S. tax system appears to discriminate against risky assets and in favor of safe assets. The discrimination depends on the type of investment and the manner in which an investor holds it. An asset held in a defined-contribution pension account is not taxed at the personal level. Corporate debt, a relatively safe asset, is deducted at the corporate level, with the implication that income generated by such assets is not taxed. However, income generated by equity investments is taxed at the firm level through taxes on corporate income.

For assets held outside of pension accounts, we need to include the taxation of personal income. At the personal level, dividends and interest income are taxed at the same rate, but capital gains have often been taxed at a lower rate. Because the tax rate on corporate income is close to or exceeds the tax rate on personal income, investment in a risky equity held outside tax-favored accounts is apparently taxed at a higher rate than safe debt. Those observations indicate that the current income tax system produces substantial discrimination against risky assets and the investments behind them, no matter how they are held by investors. Hubbard (1993) reviews conventional treatments of these issues.

Hamilton's Model of Risk and Asset Taxation. There have been many analyses of taxation and risk. Domar and Musgrave (1944) argue that an income tax increases risk taking in the economy. However, the Domar-Musgrave position is substantially altered in a general equilibrium context because many risks that a government faces will ultimately be passed on to private agents. Eaton (1981), Gordon (1985), Hamilton (1987), and Kaplow (1994) have also analyzed theoretical issues concerning tax systems and risk taking.

Unfortunately, quantitative analyses of taxation generally ignore risk—unsurprisingly, because incorporating risk in dynamic general equilibrium analysis is difficult. It is also unclear how we should calibrate any such model: we do not understand why there is such a large gap between the mean return of safe and risky assets. However, we should not totally ignore risk in tax reform analyses. We use Hamilton's (1987) model to examine the impact of differential taxation because it focuses on the most basic elements of asset allocation and risk. The model allows us to compare consumption taxation, uniform income taxation, and differential income taxation in one model.

We assume that two types of investment projects exist. We assume that the net income from risky assets is taxed at rate τ_Z and the income from the safe assets is taxed at rate τ_R. We assume that agents have a constant relative risk-aversion utility function[12] and discount the future at the rate of 4 percent per year.

Further, we assume that all revenues are rebated lump sum to investors. We make the common assumption to abstract from government expenditures policies. In this stochastic context, the assumption takes on added importance. If revenues were destroyed, then a constant income tax, as Domar and Musgrave (1994) have argued, would shift investment toward the risky asset. However, we find that assumption unrealistic—government expenditures do not immediately react to revenue shocks. The essential idea behind the assumption is that current revenue shocks lead either to tax cuts or to an increase in government expenditures on goods that are appropriate substitutes for private consumption. We do not argue that this is the most valid specification of actual policies, but use it because it is one that allows an examination of the critical issues without modeling fine details of government expenditure policies.

Utility and Revenue. We use Hamilton's model to examine the trade-off between utility and revenue. We examine several numerical cases. First, we assume that the risky asset has a mean return of 10 percent and a standard deviation of 25 percent and that the safe asset has a mean return of 1 percent. We do not defend this particular assumption. In any case, after the examples below have been recalculated for alternative means and variances, we find that the qualitative points are unchanged.

Hamilton (1987) examines optimal income taxation in such models. He shows that the optimal constant tax policy has equal tax rates for safe and risky assets. We examine the global trade-offs among various nonoptimal tax policies.

Figure 2–4 displays important features for relative risk aversion of 10 (corresponding to $\gamma = .1$ in table 2–2). The case may appear to imply great risk aversion. However, some implications are reasonable. In particular, the standard deviations of consumption and output are about 1 percent, which is close to observed values.

Figure 2–4 presents two types of curves relating the tax on the safe asset, τ_R, and the tax on the risky asset, τ_Z. The curves U_1, U_3, and U_5 are isoutility curves corresponding to the cases where $\tau_R = \tau_Z = .1, .3, .5$. That is, any combination of taxes along U_1 produces the same expected utility as the tax policy $\tau_R = \tau_Z = .1$. Expected utility is greater as we move south and west. Similarly, R_1, R_3, and R_5 are the isorevenue curves corresponding to the cases where $\tau_R = \tau_Z = .1, .3, .5$. The dotted line is the 45-degree line. Revenue increases as we move east and north. A consumption tax is represented at the origin where $\tau_R = \tau_Z = 0$. The isorevenue and isoutility curves are tangent along the 45-degree line; the placement implies that the optimal policy is one

FIGURE 2–4
Revenue and Welfare Trade-Offs with Asset Taxation

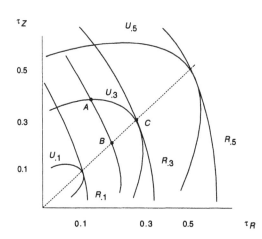

of equal tax rates, as Hamilton proved.

Although the optimality results of figure 2–4 correspond to theory, the global trade-offs are strange. Revenue is relatively insensitive to changes in the tax on risky assets. This is not too surprising because most wealth in figure 2–4 is in safe assets. More surprising is the shape of the isoutility curves away from the optimal policy. If the tax rate on safe assets is much less than the tax rate on risky assets, an increase in tax rates can keep utility unchanged or can even improve utility.

Those features of figure 2–4 show the importance of explicitly including uncertainty in the analysis. The normal procedure would insert the average pre-tax and post-tax returns into formulas for utility and revenue in a deterministic model. The approximation would incorrectly predict the shape of the isoutility curves because it would predict a uniform fall in utility as tax rates rise.

We can use figure 2–4 to make some assessments about the value of converting to consumption taxation and of implementing other, less radical reforms. In figure 2–4, a constant tax on consumption is effectively a lump-sum tax because there is no decision about the labor supply. We proceed under the assumption that figure 2–4 approximates the welfare gain if the labor supply were slightly elastic. Suppose that $\tau_R = .15$ and $\tau_Z = .35$, the situation at point A. The utility-maximizing policy raising the same revenue, at C, implies a slight reduction in the tax on risky investments and a greater increase in the tax on safe assets. The optimal revenue neutral change is to move to point B, where utility is higher. The move from A to a consumption tax can be decomposed into two moves, first to a revenue-neutral change to a uniform tax at B and then to the origin in figure 2–4.

Analyses that ignore the differential taxation of assets miss the utility gain associated with eliminating nonuniformities, such as the move from A to B.

TABLE 2–7
Excess Burden of Taxation with Risky Assets

γ	τ_Z	τ_R	MEB_R	MEB_Z	MEB_K	DB_R	TB
.5	.1	.1	.10	.061	.056	0	.025
	.4	.1	1.90	.510	.580	.11	.220
.1	.1	.1	.01	.011	.002	0	.005
	.4	.1	-.01	.120	.037	.022	.029

That gain would be achieved even if we just integrated corporate and individual taxation. When we add that feature to the analysis, we find another benefit from moving to consumption taxation.

Table 2–7 displays the welfare cost of taxation in the Hamilton model of risk and taxation. We examine the case of $\mu = .10$, $\sigma = .25$, and $r = .01$. We assume that safe assets are taxed at a rate $\tau_R = .1$ and that risky assets are taxed at the rates $\tau_Z = .1, .4$. MEB_R is the marginal excess burden of increasing τ_R, measured as the change in the certainty equivalent for consumption per dollar of change in revenue. MEB_Z (MEB_K) is the marginal excess burden associated with raising a dollar of revenue by a slight increase in the taxation of income from risky assets (all assets). We also compute the value of major changes in taxation. To do so, we compute the change in utility, measured by the certainty equivalent of constant consumption flow. We compare that with the certainty equivalent of the change in revenue flow. The differential burden DB_R is the value per dollar of change in revenue from eliminating differential taxation. TB is the total burden of the initial system of taxation per dollar of revenue.

If $\tau_Z = \tau_R = .1$, safe and risky assets are treated symmetrically, and the total burden is small. However, the marginal burden of introducing any asymmetry is higher than the marginal burden of a uniform increase. In the $\gamma = .5$ row, the total burden of taxation is 2.5 cents, and the marginal burden of asset taxation is 5.6 cents. However, the marginal burden of raising the tax on risky assets only is 6.1 cents. When we examine the asymmetric case of $\tau_Z = .4$ and $\tau_R = .1$, the results are more striking. The gain from eliminating all taxation of asset income is 22 cents per dollar of revenue, but the gain of eliminating just the asymmetric treatment, holding fixed total revenue, is 11 cents per dollar of initial revenue. The benefits of reducing asymmetries increase substantially in that case.

Those observations apply even to those who hold their equity in 401(k) accounts or similar pension savings accounts. Individual investors still pay taxes on their risky assets through the corporate income tax. In reality, a U.S. taxpayer faces three asset categories—debt, equity, and housing—even if all financial assets are in tax-favored accounts.

The asymmetric tax treatment of assets produces a substantial burden on investors in the Hamilton model. We have examined just one particular model of taxation and risk, but it is a natural one to study. Further investigation of alternative models might be fruitful, but there is no reason to suspect that the results would be different. The main intuition is clear: if the elasticity of demand for consumption is the same across all states (as assumed in Hamilton), no rationale exists for the asymmetric treatment of income across states. The asymmetric treatment of assets by the U.S. tax code only reduces the efficiency of the U.S. economy.

Tax Policy and Formation of Human Capital

Human capital is the most important determinant of wealth and income for most individuals and for any modern economy. However, income tax analyses devote less effort to understanding the taxation of human capital than the taxation of physical capital and the labor supply. A separate treatment is necessary because human capital is neither just capital nor just part of the labor supply. We show that consideration of human capital strengthens the case for consumption taxation; essentially, the inclusion increases the elasticity of the effective labor supply and increases the responsiveness of output to asset income. We also show how such consideration raises new issues about how we implement a consumption tax.

Optimal Taxation of Investments in Human Capital and Education. Investments in education and in other aspects of human capital present special problems for tax analysis.[13] Education is an investment good because it increases labor productivity, but it may also have a consumption value. Diamond and Mirrlees (1971) argue for taxing final goods but not intermediate goods. Because human capital appears to be a mixture of the labor supply, investment, and consumption, the implications of the Diamond-Mirrlees position for human capital are unclear.

Judd 1999 examines the issues in a dynamic, general equilibrium model. The study assumes that an individual invests in both financial assets, A (which finance physical capital, k), and human capital, H. Over a lifetime, the investor earns $\bar{r}A$ in asset income where $\bar{r}$ is the after-tax return on financial assets. He also earns $\bar{w} L(H,n)$ in labor income where $L(H,n)$ is the effective units of labor input if he works n hours, his human capital is H, and $\bar{w}$ is the after-tax wage for a unit of effective labor. The investor allocates savings between financial investments and investments in human capital, x. Investments in human capital equal to x earn tax credits at rate s and have a net cost of $x (1 - s)$. The aggregate production function is $f(k, L (H, n))$ where f is a standard constant returns-to-scale production function.

The incorporation of human capital in this problem generates a tension. If we think of human capital as capital, then the logic in Judd 1985b argues against the taxation of human capital. That position leaves labor income as the only source of tax revenue in the long run. However, it is difficult to tax labor income without distorting investments in human capital. Judd 1999 shows that if human capital does not affect utility, then there should be no net taxation on the return of investment in human capital, only taxation of the hours of the labor supply. That approach can be implemented by taxing labor income while allowing the immediate deduction of all expenditures for investment in human capital. The results follow exactly the logic of Diamond and Mirrlees.[14]

Is Education Only an Intermediate Good? If H is only an intermediate good, then all investments in human capital should be expensed. But if H is also a final good—that is, $u_h > 0$—the 1999 Judd study shows that we want a positive tax on returns to human capital. Many components of an education appear to have substantial consumption value. Music appreciation courses help one enjoy symphonies and operas later. Sometimes the educational activity itself has both a productive value and an aesthetic value. For example, mathematics courses such as calculus, algebra, and topology not only teach the student highly productive skills but also introduce the student to the beauty of mathematics and the joy of solving math problems.

Comparing the financial returns of alternative assets can provide evidence about the character of education. If education has a lower financial return than comparable financial assets, then human capital must be producing some non-pecuniary utility returns, is partly a consumption good, and should be taxed. The literature has addressed the issue. Becker (1976) argues that years of education and corporate equity have roughly the same mean financial return.[15] He further argues (implicitly assuming that education has no final good value) that the parity shows no underinvestment in education.

Becker's comparison with equity raises the question of why education has as high a risk premium as equity. Some economists had argued that underinvestment existed because the return on education exceeded the return on bonds. Unfortunately, scant empirical work addresses those issues. Wage income may move with corporate profits, but wages are less cyclical than profits. Furthermore, the price of risk for human capital depends on the relationship between profits; the marginal impact of investment on human capital depends on wage riskiness. Because less educated workers are more likely to experience unemployment during a recession, education appears to reduce exposure to systematic risk. Therefore, the price of risk attached to investments in human capital appears to be less than that associated with corporate equity. In any case, comparisons with financial assets do not indicate excessive investment in years of education, nor do they indicate any consumption component to education. We proceed under the assumption that education is purely an intermediate good.

Importance of Human Capital. We next illustrate the quantitative importance of human capital for tax analyses. We consider a special case of the model described above. We assume that $L(H, n) = H^\phi n$ and $f(k, L) = k^\alpha L^{1-\alpha}$. If $\phi = 0$, we have a conventional model with only physical capital. We assume $0 < \phi < 1$, with the implication of decreasing returns to investments in human capital. As in table 2–2, let $\gamma > 0$ be the elasticity of substitution in consumption and $\eta > 0$ the elasticity of the labor supply. We highlight the importance of human capital to tax analysis by computing the elasticity of long-run output with respect to the tax and subsidy rates. More precisely, we report the percentage change in long-run output, denoted by ε_K, ε_L, and ε_s, in response to a 1 percent change in net-of-tax rates $1 - \tau_K$ and $1 - \tau_L$ on physical capital and labor income and to $1 - s$, the after-tax cost of investments in human capital.

Table 2–8 reports those elasticities for various values of the critical parameters. We assume that the level of investment in human capital equals half of investment in physical capital, a conservative choice. We choose ϕ to be .1 or .3. The choice $\phi = .3$ implies that a 10 percent increase in accumulated investments in human capital results in a 3 percent rise in wages, again a conservative choice. Otherwise, we choose values for γ and η similar to those in table 2–2.

Table 2–8 shows the importance of including human capital in the analysis. First, long-run output is sensitive to the treatment of investments in human capital. Even when $\phi = .1$, a 10 percent change in $1 - s$ alters steady-state output by about 1 percent, and the sensitivity can be half as much as the sensitivity of output to changes in the tax on labor. When $\phi = .3$, changes in the treatment of investments in human capital are as important as changes in the treatment of labor and capital income. The presence of human capital means that the supply of effective labor $H^\phi n$ is more elastic than if human capital had no marginal value. The increase in the elasticity of the labor supply increases the responsiveness of output to the taxation of asset income and the efficiency cost of the taxation of capital income.

Table 2–8 also shows that adding human capital to the analysis increases the benefits from a consumption tax. The sensitivity of output to τ_K when $\phi = .3$ is higher than when $\phi = .1$. As human capital becomes more important, benefits from reducing the taxation of capital income increase.

To understand the impact of human capital, we examine the allocation of total capital across human and physical capital. The equilibrium allocation ratio is given by

$$\frac{H}{k} = \frac{\phi}{\alpha} \frac{1}{1-\tau_K} \frac{1-\tau_L}{1-s} \qquad (2\text{-}7)$$

Equation 2–7 shows that all three tax policy tools affect the H/k ratio in quantitatively symmetric fashions.

Equation 2–7 also indicates that new issues arise when we convert from the taxation of income to the taxation of consumption. In an efficient allocation, H/k should just equal ϕ/α, the relative coefficients for factor shares of human and physical capital. According to Diamond and Mirrlees, an optimal tax policy would not deviate from that. If we have an income tax whereby $\tau_K = \tau_L$ but

TABLE 2–8
Elasticity of Long-Run Output to Net-of-Tax Rates

γ	η	$\phi = .1$			$\phi = .3$		
		ε_K	ε_L	ε_S	ε_L	ε_K	ε_S
.5	.1	.51	.21	-.11	.75	.78	-.65
.5	.5	.41	.36	-.09	.55	.84	-.47
.1	.1	.29	.12	-.07	.36	.37	-.31

investments in human capital are not expensed ($s = 0$), then the H/k ratio is efficient. However, the inverse elasticity rule says that τ_K should be zero. If we just set $\tau_K = 0$, the resulting H/k ratio would not be efficient. Efficiency would be restored if we set $s = \tau_L$, with the implication that investments in human capital should be expensed.

Tax Treatment of Investments in Human Capital. The U.S. tax code takes a mixed approach to human capital. On-the-job training and a student's own time are both effectively deductible, although expenditures such as tuition and books are generally not. Because on-the-job training and students' time are the bulk of the personal, direct expenditures on investments in human capital, some have argued that the tax system treats human capital well (see Boskin 1977 and Heckman 1976 for discussions of this issue).

However, the picture is more complex. The typical analysis treats the large expenditures made by state and local governments on education as subsidies. The Tiebout theory of excludable local goods that are publicly provided argues against this view. Local and state expenditures on education are financed primarily by local and state taxation and controlled primarily by local and state political entities. The Tiebout view contends that the costs of education are capitalized in the value of land and that public expenditures on education are effectively equivalent to private expenditures. The Tiebout view combined with this chapter's optimal tax analysis argues that all education expenditures, public and private, should be deducted from the tax base.

The presence of rationing also contradicts a pure subsidy view of education. Many college students pay tuition that is far less than the true cost—but only if they meet certain standards. A pure subsidy view ignores the nonprice rationing associated with higher education and the nonprice costs incurred by students competing for those subsidies.

The issue of how to treat educational expenditures is not a minor consideration. In fact, 1990 total expenditures on education (other than federal aid) were $370 billion, compared with $576 billion in gross investment in non-residential fixed capital. Treating educational expenditures as consumption is similar to taking away all cost recovery from investment in equipment, a proposal that would not be regarded as minor.

Although the Tiebout model is extreme, the main point is robust. In general, the citizens of most communities decide to finance the education of their children together through local taxes. In any rational model of political decisionmaking, these expenditures respond to their after-tax cost. Feldstein and Metcalf (1987) offer evidence that federal income tax rules affect local expenditures; the finding supports the approach taken here. To the extent that state and local tax deductions affect investment in human capital, some deduction is desirable.

The current federal tax code has some effect on that investment through the deductibility of state and local taxes on income and property, but that deductibility includes only a part of educational expenditures. Some parents pay substantial nondeductible tuition to send their children to private schools. The high frequency of itemization among high-income families implies a regressive tax on the accumulation of human capital. The principle of a consumption tax plus the view of human capital as an intermediate good argues for the deductibility of all such public and private expenditures in all communities.

The flat tax (see Hall and Rabushka 1983), the consumption tax (see Bradford 1986), the hybrid tax of McLure and Zodrow (1996), the USA tax (see Weidenbaum 1996), and proposals for a value-added and a national sales tax all argue for a consumption tax but define *consumption* as *income minus investment in physical capital only*. The various tax proposals differ little in their treatment of investments in human capital. The Hall-Rabushka-Armey-Forbes proposals for a flat tax would clearly allow few deductions for educational investments other than on-the-job training; the sales tax and VAT proposals are similar. The USA tax would allow limited deductibility of some educational expenses. All would eliminate the deduction for state and local taxation, which finances most educational expenditures. Conversely, the flat tax would reduce the tax rate on labor income and would thereby improve incentives for investment in human capital, as indicated in equation 2–7.

It is not immediately clear whether the current proposals for a consumption tax would hurt or would help the formation of human capital relative to the current tax system. However, the treatment of human capital is clearly important. Even if reform by means of a consumption tax did not help human capital directly, the inclusion of human capital would strengthen the case for reducing the tax burden on investment in general, as shown in table 2–8.

Distributional Concerns

This chapter has focused on aggregate output and investment and has ignored concerns about distribution. But we should address these concerns. They are not as severe as they might appear, however, and the issues regarding human capital that were addressed in the previous section suggest ways to ameliorate some of those concerns.

Workers versus Capitalists. A key feature of most of the radical tax reforms is the elimination of taxation on new investment and the reduction of taxation on the current capital stock. As a replacement, taxation on wage income and on consumption would account for much of the predicted increase in investment and output. A shift to wage taxation would seem to hurt workers. The counterargument is that the increase in capital accumulation would increase worker productivity and wages, with greater worker welfare as a result. Opponents of a consumption tax often dismiss that process as weak, slow, and indirect.

Optimal tax theory presents a strong argument for eliminating the taxation of investment income. The preceding discussion argued why the taxation of asset income damages aggregate productivity over the long run. The argument holds when we consider the impact on workers and capitalists. Judd 1985b shows that even if the government were in control of tax policy and gave workers all receipts from the taxation of asset income, it would still not tax asset income in the long run. Permanently distorting the accumulation of assets would not benefit workers because the major effect of long-run taxation of assets is the reduction of total investment and labor productivity.

The optimal tax results may appear to be solely long-run results, with little impact on the foreseeable future. We next investigate the transition process of tax reform by asking how capitalists and workers would share in tax reform with a small change in the current tax structure. Assuming that the economy[17] is in the steady state with a tax rate of τ_K on capital income and a tax credit of θ for investment,[18] table 2–9 (taken from Judd 1984) computes the change in revenue and wages from a small decrease in τ_K or a small increase in θ, with increases in wage or consumption taxation to finance any shortfall in revenue. Each dR (dW) entry in table 2–9 is the change, measured in the percentage of capital income, in the present value of the revenue from taxes on capital income, (present value of wage income), caused by a 1 percent change in τ_K or θ. If there were no change in savings, dR would equal 1 and dW would equal 0. We examine values for γ, the intertemporal elasticity of substitution in consumption, and for α, the elasticity of substitution between capital and labor. We assume that τ_K is initially either .3 or .5. We assume that θ is initially .05, representing the presence of an explicit ITC or accelerated depreciation.

The results in table 2–9 address many issues. The values for γ and σ substantially affect the magnitudes of the revenue changes. However, we do see some patterns. First, the impact on wages is often substantial. It is slight only when γ is small; those cases occur when the transition process is slow. In the other cases, a 1 percentage point decrease in τ_K or a 1 percentage point increase in θ increases wages by 0.4–1.4 percent of total capital income, a substantial change. Also, wages are affected almost equally by a 1 percent change

TABLE 2–9
Disaggregated Effects of Small Tax Changes

		$\tau_K = .3$				$\tau_K = .5$			
		Decrease τ_K		Increase θ		Decrease τ_K		Increase θ	
σ	γ	dR	dW	dR	dW	dR	dW	dR	dW
.7	1.00	-1.02	.93	-.50	1.10	-1.05	1.35	-.52	1.33
	.25	-1.01	.60	-.49	.70	-1.03	.87	-.51	.85
1.0	1.00	-.91	85	- 38	1.00	-.79	1.24	-.28	1.22
	.25	-.95	.50	-.42	.59	-.88	.74	-.36	.72
1.3	1.00	-.83	.79	-.27	.93	-.58	1.16	-.06	1.13
	.25	-.90	.44	-.37	.52	-.77	.64	-.25	.62

in either τ_K or θ. Second, changes in θ affect total revenue less than changes in τ_K. Therefore, an ITC is a much more potent tool for increasing wages and labor productivity—unsurprisingly, because an ITC affects only new investment, whereas reductions in τ_K reduce taxation of old capital as well as new investment. Table 2–9 shows that an ITC can produce the same improvement for wages at substantially less loss in revenue.

Third, increases in an ITC could be close to self-financing. The dR numbers in table 2–9 consider only revenue from taxes on capital income. When we add a reasonable tax rate for wages, we find that total revenues may rise when we increase θ. For example, consider the first line. If $\tau_K = .3$ initially, then a marginal increase in θ raises before-tax wage income by $1.10 for every $0.50 of revenue loss from the taxation of capital income. If the marginal tax rate on labor income were .45, the extra labor tax revenue would equal $0.50, and there would be no net loss in revenue. A labor tax rate of .45, which is larger than the current taxation of labor, implies that some increase in the taxation of labor would be necessary to balance the budget. If $\tau_K = .5$ initially, the second set of columns indicates that we need only a .35 marginal tax rate on labor income (a plausible description of the current tax system if we include Social Security taxes) for ITC increases to be self-financing. The possibility of self-financing ITC increases is not unusual in table 2–9. In the case of Cobb-Douglas technology ($\sigma = 1$) and log utility ($\gamma = 1.$), we need at most a .38 marginal tax rate on labor income in the example of the low initial tax rate. Self-financing decreases in τ_K are much more unusual and are plausible only with a high elasticity of substitution between capital and labor.

In any case, the substantial improvement in before-tax wages means that only a small increase in the tax rate on consumption or wages would balance the budget. More important, even if workers had to pay for an ITC increase, they would almost always be better off because dR is usually less than dW. Only when γ is substantially less than the values in table 2–9 does the revenue loss exceed the wage increases. Conversely, that situation is less likely, albeit not implausible, for reductions in τ_K.

The analysis in Judd 1984 is biased in favor of consumption taxation because of the absence of adjustment costs. However, the estimates in table 2–9 are conservative; they ignore the elements of imperfect competition, which this chapter has argued are important. In particular, if we include imperfect competition in our analysis, the $\tau_K = .5$ case in table 2–9 becomes the more relevant initial condition because table 2–3 showed that imperfect competition substantially increases the effective total tax rate on capital income.

Issues concerning distribution are important in the argument for the taxation of consumption. We have seen that the productivity-enhancing properties of even a small movement toward consumption taxation would have beneficial effects for most taxpayers, even when we consider the transition process.

Old versus Young. This chapter has used representative agent models of the economy. The approach ignores intergenerational effects by assuming that all agents live "forever" and are, effectively, the same age. An alternative paradigm often used in tax analysis is the overlapping-generations (OG) approach. Theoretical analyses such as Atkinson and Sandmo 1980 have used two-period OG models. Other studies such as Auerbach and Kotlikoff 1987 have used a version in which agents live for fifty-five periods. In such a world, people differ in age, wealth, and planning horizons. Any tax reform could affect different cohorts differently and affect future generations differently from current generations. The OG approach allows an analysis of generational issues ignored in representative agent models. We next compare these approaches and the importance of intergenerational elements for tax policy analysis.

The representative agent approach is arguably a good approximation for questions of aggregate dynamics. The issue is not that representative agent analyses literally assume that agents live forever or that agents have perfectly altruistic attitudes toward their children. The real question for aggregate analysis is the relative planning horizon of the typical agent, the flexibility in his dynamic behavior, and his view of the future. Compare, for example, the classic two-period OG model of Samuelson and the typical Auerbach-Kotlikoff (AK) model. In the Samuelson model, each agent lives for only two periods, youth and old age. If we were to interpret the Samuelson model, we would have to say that each agent at age twenty chooses a constant consumption demand and labor supply for twenty-five years, and then at age forty-five the individual can change those levels to others that are constant for the next twenty-five years or so. Such inflexibility is clearly unrealistic. In the AK version, each agent is economically active for fifty-five distinct periods (modeling ages twenty through seventy-five) and can change consumption and labor decisions each year. The extra flexibility in the AK version makes it a much more realistic model. The extra flexibility produces much more sensible descriptions of the transition process after a tax reform and allows us to use empirical analyses that similarly assume annual or similarly frequent observations of agents' decisions.

The key difference between the AK model and a representative agent model is the length of the life of the typical agent. But the importance of that difference is not clear, given the level of discounting typically used. Both Auerbach and Kotlikoff and those who use representative agent models assume that agents discount the future at an annual rate of 4 percent or thereabouts. Implicitly, then, a young person at age twenty treats a dollar at age seventy-five as being equal to 12 cents at age twenty. The utility derived between ages twenty and seventy-five is 88 percent of lifetime utility for an infinitely lived agent and 100 percent of lifetime utility in the AK model in the absence of a bequest motive.

The representative agent and AK models predict similar aggregate output and dynamics. For any fixed utility function and production function, the two models differ, but we know neither tastes nor technology with precision. The ranges of predictions of the two models are similar once we examine the wide range of empirically sensible specifications for taste and technology.

The major difference lies in the implications for specific individuals. The undisputed advantage of the AK model is its utility for analyses of intergenerational distribution. Using the AK model, Auerbach (1996) raises important concerns about the intergenerational impact of tax reform. A transition to a consumption tax would cause older taxpayers to pay a new tax on their accumulated savings (either through consumption taxation of the proceeds of asset sales or through a fall in the market value of their assets), but they would not live long enough to enjoy the benefits.

How we should interpret the Auerbach 1996 results is unclear. Consider the demographic structure of the AK model. It assumes that everyone dies at age seventy-five. These demographic assumptions are inaccurate on two accounts. First, death is an uncertain process,[19] many people live longer than seventy-five years. Table 2–10 compares life expectancies in the AK model and in the United States. In fact, in the United States, a seventy-five-year-old has a life expectancy of eleven years, not one. When an AK model says that a seventy-five-year-old loses from a tax reform because of a drop in asset prices, that loss presumably occurs because his life expectancy is just one year. If that AK model predicts that anyone younger than sixty gains, that is presumably because anyone with more than a fifteen-year life expectancy gains and that those people gain because any immediate short-run loss is balanced by gains over the following fifteen years. When we translate this interpretation to U.S.

TABLE 2–10
Life Expectancy in AK Model and the United States

| | AK Model | | U.S. Adult Population | |
Age	Life expectancy	Fraction older	Life expectancy	Fraction older
55	21	.32	25.1	.29
60	16	.24	21.1	.23
65	11	.16	17.4	.18
67	7	.13	16.1	.16
70	6	.08	14.1	.13
75	1	.01	11.0	.08
80	NA	NA	8.3	.04
85+	NA	NA	6.1	.02

Source: Commerce 1988, table 119.

demographics, the AK model apparently predicts that anyone younger than sixty-seven gains because a sixty-seven-year-old has about a sixteen-year life expectancy in the United States.

The second, and more important, difference between the AK demographic specifications and U.S. demographics is the distribution of life expectancy. Suppose that the AK model predicts that all individuals older than sixty suffer financial losses. That segment encompasses 24 percent of the population, a sizable voting bloc. Auerbach (1996) argues that transition relief to compensate those individuals would substantially limit the possible long-run gains from tax reform. That conclusion is not surprising, given the many individuals who would be harmed. Also, the AK analysis assumes that a large fraction of the population would be substantially harmed. For example, 8 percent of the population in the AK model have less than a six-year life expectancy. Compensating them would be particularly difficult because the available horizon is so short.

The U.S. demographic situation is not as grim and does not present as great a challenge to relief efforts during transition. More precisely, only those older than sixty-seven have less than a sixteen-year life expectancy, and they constitute only 16 percent of the population, not the 24 percent in the AK analysis. The smaller size of the affected population would make it easier to construct compensatory policies. Also, far fewer are substantially affected. For example, those with only a six-year life expectancy would likely suffer greater losses than the average loser; they make up 8 percent of the population in the AK model but only 2 percent in the United States.

The issue becomes even more ambiguous when we add marriage to the analysis. For example, suppose that a husband and a wife each have a life expectancy of fifteen years. If some altruism exists between husband and wife, then the effective household life expectancy is greater than fifteen.

Our analysis of asset prices with imperfect competition is also relevant here. When we add imperfect competition to the analysis, the switch to a tax on consumption would reduce asset prices by less because of the increase in pure profits to producers. We should consider other implications of tax reform. Auerbach (1996) assumes that capital gains are taxed in an accrued fashion. In reality, older taxpayers would hold considerable amounts of equity with large unrealized gains. Reform by a consumption tax would mean forgiving the unpaid taxes on those unrealized capital gains. In fact, by integrating the reduction in the taxation of capital gains with any reasonable fall in asset prices, an older taxpayer might enjoy a gain in disposable income.

Both the representative agent and the overlapping-generations models are highly stylized, with important differences in their demographic structure. Overlapping-generations models can analyze issues of intergenerational incidence. However, those incidence results would be sensitive to the demographic and tax policy details. The conclusions of analyses such as Auerbach 1996 seem overly pessimistic.

Middle-Income versus Upper-Income. One of the unfortunate features of many proposals for a consumption tax is the relatively slight gain for middle-income groups, whereas upper-income groups gain much more in the short run. The reasons are clear. Middle-income taxpayers lose key deductions, such as the ones for home mortgage interest and state and local taxes. The reduction in the taxation of asset income is of less value to them because most of their assets are already in tax-favored vehicles, such as owner-occupied housing and pension funds. Their ability to shelter asset income is growing under the current system as we increase the scope, size, and liquidity of those special accounts. Upper-income groups benefit more from the rate reductions and the elimination of asset-income taxation because their savings exceed the contribution limits of pension accounts.

Reform proposals for a consumption tax need to be altered to form the necessary political coalition. One alternative is to keep the deduction for mortgage interest, but that adjustment would be bad news for resource allocation. One of the primary benefits of the flat tax and similar proposals would be the elimination of the current bias toward housing investment and against nonresidential business fixed investment. Because the housing stock is roughly the same size as other forms of capital, such a reallocation of investment would substantially improve economic efficiency in the long run. If we maintained the deduction for mortgage interest in the long run, we would be losing one of the primary benefits of the flat tax.

TABLE 2–11
Major Tax Expenditures, 1998
(estimated billions of dollars)

Home mortgage interest deductions	51.2
State and local taxes deductions	
Owner-occupied housing	17.7
Other nonbusiness deductions	32.1

SOURCE: Commerce 1998, table 544.

An alternative is to allow some deductions for state and local taxes, possibly tied to educational expenditures. That adjustment would redirect some tax relief to the middle class and would be no worse in terms of simplicity than allowing some form of deduction for mortgage interest. The incidence would be similar to the deduction of mortgage interest because both are strongly related to income. Allowing some deductions tied to education would be consistent with the principles of consumption taxation, whereas the deduction for mortgage interest clearly violates the conceptual foundations of consumption taxation.

Table 2–11 displays the estimated costs to tax revenue from various deductions in the current tax system. The revenue cost from the deduction for home mortgage interest roughly equals the revenue loss from the deductions by households for state and local taxes. The size of these tax expenditures reflects the current marginal tax rate. The actual revenue loss would be less under a flat tax with a marginal rate of 20 percent or less. The deductions for mortgage interest and for state and local taxes appear to have roughly the same budgetary consequences. They probably have similar impacts on distribution. The benefits of the deduction for mortgage interest is perhaps more focused on the middle class because the deduction is capped and because the top income groups spend less of their income on housing than the middle class. Of course, any deduction for mortgage interest included in a proposal for a modified flat tax would probably also be capped, with the implication that a cap on deductions for state and local taxes would add no greater complexity than a capped deduction for mortgage interest.

This chapter has focused on the educational expenditures of state and local government. Although education is the major expenditure of state and local government, a deduction tied to those expenditures would be smaller than the current deduction for state and local taxes. This study has argued that education is an intermediate good whether financed privately or through local governmental entities, and that its tax treatment should not depend on the organizational form that individuals decide to use. This argument suggests that we ask the same question of other public services, such as police, fire, and the judicial system. If they are intermediate goods, then they too should be excluded from a base for a consumption tax.

A far more detailed examination is needed of the nature and the allocation of goods provided by local governments. Such an analysis should produce proposals that deal with the problems of transition and distribution without deviating much from the underlying goals of consumption taxation.

Conclusions

Economists have argued that switching to a consumption tax would generate large long-run gains, although some have argued that difficult problems regarding distribution and transition would occur. Earlier arguments have been unduly pessimistic because they have ignored many important elements. Including some features of the U.S. economy that make it modern and technologically advanced (such as imperfect competition, the accumulation of human capital, and risk) substantially strengthens the case for a consumption tax.

Imperfect competition—a ubiquitous feature of a modern economy—acts as a tax on the U.S. economy. This study has shown that the feature is particularly damaging in the investment goods sector. Innovation in intermediate goods is financed by allowing imperfect competition in the industries that produce intermediate goods. Such imperfect competition reduces the productive efficiency of the economy. Any tax on capital income inflicts even more damage on the incentive of the economy to make desirable investments. This chapter has shown that the gains from eliminating the tax burden on capital income are particularly great.

The current tax system discriminates against risk-taking because equity-financed investments pay more taxes than debt-financed investments. That bias has no rational purpose and distorts the allocation of capital. Analyses that ignore that feature of the current tax system substantially underestimate the value of moving to a consumption tax or of more modest integration proposals.

Human capital is an important part of any modern economy and makes labor productivity more sensitive to tax policy. Moving to a tax on consumption would not only increase investment in physical capital but would also increase wages and the incentive to invest in education and other forms of human capital—and would thus produce an even greater increase in long-run output.

Those considerations dramatically affect the estimates of the benefits of moving to a tax on consumption. Overall, incorporating those elements into an analysis would easily double and often triple estimates of the long-run benefits. Those new considerations would also help with the problems of transition. The effects of imperfect competition would push up stock market values and would reduce any adverse effects of tax reform for older taxpayers. This chapter also argues that a realistic view of life expectancy would likewise alleviate concerns about intergenerational equity. When we consider the role of education as an investment, we see that deductions for educational expenditures may be used to reduce middle-class losses from tax reform without continuing the inefficient preference for owner-occupied housing.

At a more fundamental level, this study argues that a proper understanding of tax systems shows that an income tax is a particularly bad form of taxation and that the current tax system violates most principles of sound tax policy. The choice of tax systems is an important and difficult one, but the case for efficient taxation of consumption, as embodied in various current proposals, is strong and growing stronger.

Notes

1.   A semantic problem can arise in discussing the taxation and nontaxation of asset income. In this chapter, any comment on whether a tax system taxes asset income implicitly refers to the effective tax rate on new investment. In this sense, the current tax system taxes asset income, but the Hall-Rabushka flat tax and most other proposals for a consumption tax do not tax asset income.

2.   See Aaron, Galper, and Pechman 1988 for a description of the problems of a hybrid tax system.

3.   See Atkinson and Stiglitz 1972 and Atkinson and Sandmo 1980 for formal presentations of optimal taxation theory.

4.   This chapter ignores supply elasticities because they are not as relevant for these applications of the inverse elasticity rule.

5.   Simulations of tax policy analysis may stumble on this if they assume tastes that lead to time-varying elasticities of consumption demand.

6.   See Judd 1987 for a long list of empirically estimated elasticities of the labor supply and tax rates of labor used there to compute *MEB*.

7.   A model with heterogeneous capital goods would demonstrate better points about productive efficiency. The more general analysis in Judd 1997 indicates that such models strongly support those conclusions.

8.   The quantity is small but typical for competitive models. An alternative way to express the welfare gain is to report the ratio of welfare gain to the revenue or revenue change. However, that index is sensitive to details such as the standard deduction. The index used in this chapter is a cleaner way to express the welfare gains, and it allows us to ignore irrelevant details.

9.   Labor taxation is ignored because labor is inelastically supplied in this simple analysis. However, the presence of a wage tax with an elastic labor supply generally increases the welfare costs of taxation. Hence, this study's results are conservative estimates of welfare costs.

10. We always assume perfect competition in financial markets. We argue that no firm embodies a substantial share of all outstanding equity and no firm offers a substantially unique risk opportunity.

11. In a richer model, different firms would sell different goods and would experience different changes in asset prices. For example, those firms specializing in capital goods would experience an immediate increase in demand whereas those specializing in consumer goods would lose sales because the consumption share of output falls in the short run. However, the assumption that all investors are well diversified permits a focus on aggregate values of assets.

12. More precisely, we assume $u(c) = \dfrac{c^{1-1/\gamma}}{1 - 1/\gamma}$

where γ is also the intertemporal elasticity of consumption used in Table 2–2.

13. Many forms of investment in human capital exist. This chapter focuses on education and on-the-job training because they are most relevant for tax analyses. Other forms of human capital investment, such as child care and medical care, are even more difficult to analyze.

14. There have been other analyses of human capital and taxation in economic growth models. Jones, Manuelli, and Rossi (1997) argue that there should be no taxation of anything in the long run. That extreme position arises from special assumptions about functional form made to arrive at a model with a constant growth rate in consumption and all forms of investment. Judd (1999) examines a strictly more general model.

15. Those are estimates of the social return to education, including any social expenditure as well as the direct monetary and time inputs of students. Although there has been much effort to refine the estimates of the return to years of education, the Becker findings are in the middle range of current estimates, particularly if one adds fringe benefits and other nonwage benefits of education.

16. These parameter values are also conservative when compared with a common assumption of $\phi = 1$ in the endogenous growth literature.

17. As in table 2–2, we assume a representative agent model with an inelastic labor supply.

18. The investment tax credit proxies for any investment incentive above economic depreciation. In particular, the credit proxies for accelerated depreciation as well as an explicit ITC. We assume here that the ITC is on all investment, not just equipment. The assumption is consistent with the nature of proposals for a consumption tax.

19. This chapter assumes that there is an actuarially fair annuity market. If such markets did not exist, then an income tax may be desirable as a way to share life-expectancy risk. In general, when capital markets are not perfect, income taxation may dominate consumption taxation. See Hubbard and Judd

1986, 1987, and 1988 for analyses of taxation with capital market imperfections. Future work should integrate the considerations of Hubbard and Judd with the concerns of this chapter to determine the relative strength of the conflicting forces.

References

Aaron, Henry J., Harvey Galper, and Joseph Pechman, eds. 1988. *Uneasy Compromise: Problems of a Hybrid Income-Consumption Tax.* Washington, D.C.: Brookings Institution.

Appelbaum, E. 1982. "The Estimation of the Degree of Oligopoly Power." *Journal of Econometrics* 19: 287–99.

Atkinson, A., and J. Stiglitz. 1972. "The Structure of Indirect Taxation and Economic Efficiency." *Journal of Public Economics* 1:97–119.

Atkinson, Anthony B., and Agnar Sandmo. 1980. "Welfare Implications of the Taxation of Savings." *Economic Journal* 90 (September): 529–49.

Auerbach, Alan J. 1979. "The Optimal Taxation of Heterogeneous Capital." *Quarterly Journal of Economics* 93: 589–612.

————. 1989. "The Deadweight Loss from 'Non-neutral' Capital Income Taxation." *Journal of Public Economics* 40 (October): 1–36.

————. 1996. "Tax Reform, Capital Accumulation, Efficiency, and Growth." In *Economic Effects of Fundamental Tax Reform,* edited by Henry J. Aaron and William G. Gale. Washington, D.C.: Brookings Institution.

Auerbach, Alan J., and L. Kotlikoff. 1987. *Dynamic Fiscal Policy.* Cambridge: Cambridge University Press.

Balcer, Y., I. Garfinkel, K. Krynski, and E. Sadka. 1983. "Income Redistribution and the Structure of Indirect Taxation." In *Social Policy Evaluation: An Economic Perspective,* edited by E. Helpman, A. Razin, and E. Sadka. New York: Academic Press.

Barro, Robert J., and Xavier Sala-I-Martin. 1995. *Economic Growth.* New York: McGraw-Hill.

Becker, Gary. 1976. *Human Capital: A Theoretical and Empirical Analysis.* Chicago: University of Chicago Press.

Boskin, M. 1977. "Notes on the Tax Treatment of Human Capital." In U.S. Department of Treasury, Office of Tax Analysis, Conference on Tax Research 1975. Washington, D.C.: Government Printing Office.

Bradford, D. 1986. *Untangling the Income Tax.* Cambridge: Harvard University. Press,

Diamond, P. A. 1973. "Taxation and Public Production in a Growth Setting." In *Models of Economic Growth,* edited by J. A. Mirrlees and N. H. Stern. London: Macmillan.

Diamond, P. A., and J. A. Mirrlees. 1971. "Optimal Taxation and Public Production." *American Economic Review* 61: 8–27, 261–78.

Domar, Evsey D., and Richard A. Musgrave. 1944. "Proportional

Income Taxation and Risk-Taking." *Quarterly Journal of Economics* 58 (May): 388–422.

Domowitz, Ian, R. Glenn Hubbard, and Bruce C. Petersen. 1986a. "Business Cycles and the Relationship between Concentration and Price-Cost Margins." *Rand Journal of Economics* 17 (spring): 1–17.

————. 1986b. "The Intertemporal Stability of the Concentration Margins Relationship." *Journal of Industrial Economics* 35 (September): 13–34.

————. 1988. "Market Structure and Cyclical Fluctuations in U.S. Manufacturing." *Review of Economics and Statistics* 70 (1) (February):55–66.

Eaton, J. 1981. "Fiscal Policy, Inflation and the Accumulation of Risky Capital." *Review of Economic Studies* 48: 435–45.

Feldstein, Martin S. 1978. "The Rate of Return, Taxation and Personal Savings." *Economic Journal* 88: 482–87.

Feldstein, Martin S., and G. E. Metcalf. 1987. "The Effect of Federal Tax Deductibility on State and Local Taxes and Spending." *Journal of Political Economy* 95: 710–36.

Gordon, Roger H. 1985. "Taxation of Corporate Capital Income: Tax Revenues versus Tax Distortions." *Quarterly Journal of Economics* 100: 1–27.

Goulder, Lawrence H., and Philippe Thalmann. 1993. "Approaches to Efficient Capital Taxation: Leveling the Playing Field vs. Living by the Golden Rule." *Journal of Public Economics* 50 (February): 169–96.

Gravelle, Jane. 1994. *The Economic Effects of Taxing Capital Income.* Cambridge: MIT Press.

————. 1995. "The Flat Tax and Other Tax Proposals: Who Will Bear the Tax Burden?" Report for Congress 95-1141E. Washington, D.C.: Congressional Research Service, November 29.

Hall, Robert E. 1986. "Market Structure and Macro Fluctuations." *Brookings Papers on Economic Activity* 2: 285–322.

Hall, Robert E., and Alvin Rabushka. 1983. *Low Tax, Simple Tax, Flat Tax.* New York: McGraw-Hill.

Hamilton, J. H. 1987. "Taxation, Savings, and Portfolio Choice in a Continuous Time Model." *Public Finance* 42: 264–82.

Heckman, James. 1976. "A Life-Cycle Model of Earnings, Learning, and Consumption." *Journal of Political Economy* 84 (4) (August): Sll–44.

Hubbard, R. Glenn. 1993. "Corporate Tax Integration: A View from the Treasury Department." *Journal of Economic Perspectives* 7 (1): 115–32.

Hubbard, R. Glenn, and Kenneth L. Judd. 1986. "Liquidity Constraints, Fiscal Policy, and Consumption." *Brookings Papers on Economic Activity* 0 (1): 1–50.

————. 1987. "Social Security and Individual Welfare: Precautionary Saving, Borrowing Constraints, and the Payroll Tax." *American Economic Review* 77 (4) (September): 630–46.

—————. 1988. "Capital Market Imperfections and Tax Policy Analysis in the Life Cycle Model." *Annales d'Economie et de Statistique* 0 (9) (January–March): 111–39.

Jones, L., R. Manuelli, and P. Rossi. 1993. "Optimal Taxation in Models of Endogenous Growth." *Journal of Political Economy* 101 (3) (June): 485–517.

Jorgenson, Dale W., and Kun Young Yun. 1990. "Tax Reform and U.S. Economic Growth." *Journal of Political Economy* 98 (5) (October): S151–93.

Judd, Kenneth L. 1984. "Redistributive and Efficiency Effects of Capital Tax Changes in a Dynamic Model." Mimeo. Northwestern University.

—————. 1985a. "On the Performance of Patents." *Econometrica* 53 (3) (May): 567–85.

—————. 1985b. "Redistributive Taxation in a Simple Perfect Foresight Model." *Journal of Public Economics* 28 (October): 59–83.

—————. 1987. "The Welfare Cost of Factor Taxation in a Perfect Foresight Model." *Journal of Political Economy* 95 (August): 675–709.

—————. 1997. "The Optimal Tax Rate for Capital Income Is Negative." National Bureau of Economic Research Working Paper 6004. Cambridge: NBER.

—————. 1999. "Optimal Taxation and Spending in General Competitive Growth Models." *Journal of Public Economics* 71 (1):1–26.

Kaplow, Louis. 1994. "Taxation and Risk Taking: A General Equilibrium Perspective." *National Tax Journal* 47: 789–98.

Kocherlakota, Narayana R. 1996. "The Equity Premium: It's Still a Puzzle." *Journal of Economic Literature* 34 (March): 42–71.

McLure, C., and G. R. Zodrow. 1996. "A Hybrid Approach to the Direct Taxation of Consumption." In *Frontiers of Tax Reform,* edited by Michael Boskin. Stanford: Hoover Institution Press.

Robinson, Joan. 1934. *The Economics of Imperfect Competition.* London: Macmillan.

U.S. Department of Commerce. 1998. *Statistical Abstract of the United States: 1998.* Washington, D.C.: Government Printing Office.

U.S. Department of the Treasury. 1992. *Integration of the Individual and Corporate Tax Systems: Taxing Business Income Once.* Washington, D. C.: Government Printing Office.

Weidenbaum, M. 1996. "The Nunn-Domenici USA Tax." In *Frontiers of Tax Reform,* edited by Michael Boskin. Stanford: Hoover Institution Press.

Commentary

Alan J. Auerbach

In his thoughtful and thought-provoking chapter, Kenneth Judd gathers arguments from many sources to support his proposition that the economic gains from adopting a consumption tax would be greater, and the economic costs less, than many others have concluded. His criticism takes two forms. First, he shows how the implications of simple competitive models without uncertainty are often overlooked. Second, he points to several realistic modifications of the simple model; their inclusion generally magnifies the net benefits of a shift to consumption taxation. Judd concludes that adopting a consumption tax should be a much easier decision than it has seemed in recent years.

In general I agree with Judd's analysis. Although I am not convinced that one can simply "add up" all additional benefits that he highlights in computing the net gains from adopting a consumption tax, he is right to warn us against drawing sweeping conclusions from simple models. Here I will review his arguments and offer my own interpretation and some suggestions on re-lated issues.

Why a Consumption Tax Should Look Good

Judd offers several arguments for consumption taxes. First, he points to an important result associated with some of his earlier work: optimal tax theory calls for no long-run distortions on the taxation of capital income. The intuition that he provides here shows why that result does not depend on the precise form of individual preferences: over time, if any distortion results from the taxation of capital income, the distortion of future consumption decisions will rise without bound. We can prevent that only by stopping the taxation of capital income at some future date. Although that result holds in full generality only in an infinite-horizon model, the result would not differ much for the long planning horizon typically assumed in life-cycle models. The result here cuts the Gordian knot of second-best theory and urges us to push on. However, such a result is already implicit in the existing estimates based on optimizing models, such as the one Judd cited here (Auerbach 1996). Thus, his argument is really a reminder of what underlies some efficiency gains from consumption taxation found in the existing literature. But Judd argues that we often ignore many other gains.

1. *Production inefficiency.* Judd reminds us of another result from optimal tax theory, the production efficiency theorem of Diamond-Mirrlees, which says that we should tax only final purchases and thereby avoid distortions to the production process itself. Because, in the context of a dynamic model, one can view consumption at different dates as different consumption goods, the

Diamond-Mirrlees result does not rule out uniform taxes on capital income. But taxes on capital income are not uniform; they impose different burdens on different types of assets. Still, one should not count eliminating all that as a potential gain from moving to a consumption tax. We may not be able to eliminate all such interasset distortions without eliminating taxes on capital income—a key argument of some advocates of a consumption tax—but lately we have not tried to do so very diligently. Tax-free imputed rent, favorable tax rates for capital gains, and the alternative minimum tax are all major examples of self-inflicted distortions. They are not inevitable parts of an income tax.

2. *Imperfect competition.* Citing no less a source than Joan Robinson, Judd argues that we should subsidize firms that produce capital goods and that are imperfectly competitive, to bring their prices down to marginal cost. (He argues that we should not worry much about such subsidization because even with inefficiently high prices, monopoly rents are small, as would be true under Robinson's version of imperfect competition. I say more on this below.) Thus, reducing taxes on capital income, which further discourage the use of capital, offers an even greater benefit. The most intuitive way to see that point is to think of such additional distortions in terms of their impact on consumption decisions. Like explicit taxes on capital income, they distort future consumption. Thus, when we evaluate the benefits of reducing taxes on capital income, we should measure the benefits starting from a more distorted point. Given the familiar lesson in public finance—that distortions rise with the square of the overall wedge—eliminating a tax on capital income of a given size provides much more benefit when another distortion is present at the same margin.

3. *Risky assets.* Some distortions among assets are associated with the risk characteristics of these assets. For example, if a corporation can finance only safe assets with tax-favored debt, then risky assets face a higher tax burden. Likewise, the asymmetric treatment of gains and losses does more damage to firms with risky investment returns. Thus, the interasset distortions already discussed are magnified when assets differ in their risk characteristics. This is a valid point, to which I offer the same caveat given above: Why should we count as a benefit of moving to consumption taxation the elimination of distortions that are imposed on us by the political process rather than by the income tax?

4. *Human capital.* As Judd emphasizes, the measured stock of capital becomes much larger once we include human capital. Hence, the potential distortions facing capital accumulation grow as well. That said, we might look at the treatment of human capital and ask what the problem is. Human capital already receives close to cash-flow tax treatment already, as foregone wages are implicitly expensed (the opportunity cost being the after-tax wage) and employer training costs are explicitly expensed. However, two problems remain. First, as the chapter points out, because some costs of education

(tuition, for example) are not deducted, the current tax system does discourage the accumulation of human capital. Conversely, the still favorable treatment of human capital encourages inefficient substitution of human capital for physical capital in production and thereby adds another layer to the picture of interasset distortion painted above. A move to consumption taxes would eliminate both the existing distortions facing the accumulation of human capital and the distortion between human and physical capital.

Of course, complications arise if some "investment in human capital" is really consumption, as a good share of the expenditure on college education surely is. Under a true consumption tax, these expenditures would be taxed. Thus, we cannot be sure that the tax treatment of education would be more favorable under a consumption tax than at present. That possibility, in turn, raises interesting questions about whether spending on education offers additional benefits, either in the form of social externalities or in terms of the impact on income distribution. Whether such additional benefits are present or not, one must wonder about the political feasibility of a tax reform that would sharply reduce the tax burden on capital while raising the tax burden on education.

Why a Consumption Tax Shouldn't Look So Bad

Although Judd devotes more time to touting the benefits of consumption taxation, he also attempts to comfort those who fear the effects of the reform's transition.

1. *Uncertain lifetimes.* A major source of the consumption tax's efficiency gain comes from the capital levy that it would impose on initial asset holders. Those who were not too old at the onset of transition would have time to recover by taking advantage of the higher after-tax returns to investment under the new regime. But those with a short life expectancy would lose. Judd argues that simulations based on deterministic models (like mine) understate the age threshold for losing out under a tax reform because those of a relatively advanced age may live even longer. Although I agree with his point, whether that understatement changes the model's conclusions regarding the efficiency costs of compensating losers is not clear. The class of such losers in the model simulations may begin at too young an age to do so. But that age group represents a smaller fraction of the population in the model than in the real world precisely because the model lacks the property of extended life expectancy.

Conversely, the presence of lifetime uncertainty might impart at least one beneficial attribute to the capital levy, that of insurance. Absent a perfect annuities market, some precautionary saving must be done to ensure against the income risk of outliving one's resources. Under a shift to consumption taxation, an increase in the after-tax rate of return would accompany the capital levy. Thus, the net cost would fall with the length of life. An implicit insurance component would result, with the greatest burden imposed on those with "positive" draws—those who died soon and did not need to spread out their resources. (The wisdom of this outcome is likely to be more evident to economists than to others.)

2. *Imperfect competition.* The capital levy might have less impact on asset values if not all assets received more favorable treatment under the new system. That would be true for imperfect competition rents. Here Judd is a bit inconsistent, since he argued earlier that such rents were not large. Of course, even under competitive conditions, some sources of income, including intangible capital, might not face a capital levy. Because the current tax system already treats such capital as consumption (or better), a shift to consumption taxation would not reduce the value of existing capital relative to new capital. However, the blessing is not unmixed. Whether the reduction in the capital levy were associated with noncompetitive rents or competitive quasi-rents, the benefit for owners of existing capital would reduce the efficiency gain from the reform: taking less money away from existing asset owners would reduce the lump-sum portion of the consumption tax. Thus, if existing analyses overstated the size of the capital levy, then the efficiency gain of the consumption tax would likewise be overstated. The magnitude of the existing capital levy may be a guide to how much additional transition relief might be politically necessary, but it does not alter the fundamental trade-off between limiting capital losses and protecting efficiency gains.

Where Does That Leave Us?

This chapter has reminded us that simple models give simple results. But having started along this path, we might wish to go a bit further. One central premise common to the simple models and to the more refined versions that Judd advocates is rational long-horizon saving behavior, dictated by stable preferences over consumption at different dates and states of the world. In such a world, justifying mandatory public or employer pensions or individual retirement accounts is sometimes difficult; typically, treating all saving uniformly is preferable. Although that rational model of saving has served well as a baseline paradigm for analysis, its empirical support is not sufficiently strong that we should rule out other, perhaps less precise, alternatives. Variations in that direction seem at least as important as some raised in the chapter.

But even if we conclude that the world would be a much more efficient place under a simple, broad-based, low-rate tax on consumption, what does that conclusion imply for the direction of tax reform? As stressed above, many distortions of the income tax have little to do with the fact that we tax income rather than consumption. We ought to remember that any new consumption tax would be installed by a government that, in a single recent act of tax reform, managed to give us such jewels of tax policy as the Roth IRA, the Hope scholarship, and innumerable tax rates on capital gains.

3

Asset Price Effects of Fundamental Tax Reform

*Andrew B. Lyon
and
Peter R. Merrill*

I n recent years, a variety of legislative proposals to replace the federal income tax system with a consumption-based tax have been introduced in Congress and have been widely discussed both in the general media and among tax scholars. Leading proposals include the Armey flat tax, the Schaefer-Tauzin national retail sales tax (NST), the Nunn-Domenici unlimited savings allowance (USA) tax, the Danforth-Boren business activities tax, and the Gibbons subtraction-method value-added tax (VAT).

Such proposed reforms virtually amount to a revolution in tax policy for the United States. This chapter addresses one of the most serious concerns raised by the proposals: Would a shift to a consumption-based tax cause a significant decline in the value of existing physical capital assets and, along with it, a precipitous drop in the stock market?

al reflect the views of PricewaterhouseCoopers LLP and its partners. The authors gratefully acknowledge the assistance of Chris Edwards and Melbert Schwarz and helpful comments from Kevin Hassett, Jim Hines, and Glenn Hubbard.

Recent discussion of replacing the existing tax code with a consumption tax has suggested that a major burden of the new tax would fall on the owners of existing capital and that these owners would suffer a significant reduction in the value of their assets. For example, Jane Gravelle (1995) states that the Hall-Rabushka flat tax would cause a 20–30 percent decline in the stock market. Analyses by David Bradford (1996) and Robert Hall (1996) find similar reductions in the value of existing wealth. Yet, with the exception of the USA tax, the proposals ignore any need to address the effects of a transition on wealth, at either the business or individual levels.

Our conclusion is very different. Yes, some existing assets would experience a decline in value. But generalizations are seriously misleading. Some assets would actually increase in value, and the impact of the change in tax systems would vary widely among both firms and types of assets. As for the stock market, the market value of a firm is affected not only by the valuation of its physical assets, but also by estimates of future after-tax earnings arising from growth opportunities and the value of intangible assets, such as brand names and patents.

A simple example shows why many assets would increase in value under a revenue-neutral consumption tax. Consider the value of a patent developed through research and development; the R&D costs are deducted immediately for tax purposes under the existing income tax. In the absence of tax reform, revenues generated by an existing patent are subject to a 35 percent tax rate when earned by a corporation. Under the Armey flat tax, the revenues generated by the patent would be taxed at only a 20 percent tax rate.[1] The switch to a flat tax would increase the after-tax cash flows attributable to the patent from 65 cents per dollar of revenue to 80 cents, a 23 percent increase. Given no other changes, the value of the patent increases by 23 percent.

Although proposals for a consumption tax affect taxes at both the corporate and the individual levels, the focus here is on the effects on asset prices resulting from changes in taxation at the corporate level. This analysis suggests that declines in market value from a switch to a consumption tax would likely be much less than suggested by prior studies and might even be positive. Three factors account for the differences in our analysis:[2]

- First, a significant portion of firm value is attributable to intangible capital and growth opportunities. As the simple example above shows, the value of these assets would increase if the flat tax provided a lower statutory rate than the current income tax.
- Second, under common assumptions, an asset that was provided depreciation allowances based on economic depreciation at each point in time would decline in value in a switch to a consumption tax. However, the actual pattern of depreciation deductions provided for equipment and structures in the United States does not resemble economic depreciation.

Based on the actual system of depreciation deductions, assets would generally decline less than they would under economic depreciation, and many physical assets actually would increase in value—as is the case for intangible assets—following a switch to a consumption tax.

- Third, analyses predicting a decline in the value of existing depreciable assets assume an immediate expansion of the capital stock to its long-run equilibrium value under a consumption tax. But this expansion would not immediately occur. A variety of adjustment costs (additional costs incurred when investment is accelerated) would limit the expansion of the capital stock and would thereby reduce downward pressure on existing depreciable assets.

Experience with major tax reform proposals, such as the Tax Reform Act of 1986, suggests that Congress might ultimately provide extensive transition rules, both to minimize disruptions to the economy and to garner political support for reform. This chapter later considers the economic and political issues behind transition rules to redress windfall gains or losses.[3] The following section reviews the economic theory how a transition to a consumption tax may affect asset prices. Next, asset price effects are quantified for different property types under alternative assumptions about the adjustment process. Other transitional issues concerning businesses are then considered.[4] Finally, we evaluate the extent to which wealth effects would be for mitigated by two options for transition relief that provide the deduction of unrecovered basis in assets acquired prior to tax reform.

Asset Prices and the Value of the Firm

The analysis here is primarily concerned with the underlying market value of the assets that constitute a corporation. The total market value of a firm at time t, V_t, constituting the value of the firm's common stock and other obligations, can be defined as the value of its physical assets in place (KPt) plus the value of intangible assets (KI_t), comprised of the value of future rents and growth opportunities attributable to unique intangible assets of the firm, plus any errors in the estimation of these values (e_t):

$$V_t = KP_t + KI_t + e_t \qquad (3\text{--}1)$$

The importance of intangible assets to firm value hardly receives any consideration because these assets are not generally valued in financial statements. For many firms, however, the value of intangible assets significantly dwarfs the value of the physical assets in place. For example, in February 2000, 65 percent of the firms in the Standard & Poor's 500 index had a stock market value-to-book ratio of two or more, and more than 25 percent had a market-to-book ratio of five or more.[5] Much of the difference between these companies' stock market value and their value for financial statement purposes may be attributable to intangible assets. Valuable intangible assets include patents, know-how, trademarks, reputations, and skilled employees. As we show, a shift to consumption taxation can affect the value of a company's tangible and intangible assets quite differently.

The role of errors in valuation by investors is also important in considering how tax reform affects stock market values. Changes in the value of the firm's underlying assets and growth opportunities do not mechanically translate into changes in the market value of the firm. Investors must correctly incorporate the changes in asset valuation into security prices. For this reason, we limit our analysis to predicting how fundamental tax reform would affect underlying asset values.

A Decline in Asset Prices under a Consumption Tax? Could a tax reform replacing the corporate income tax with a cash-flow tax—a system that allows the purchase of new capital goods as an immediate write-off—be anything but unambiguously good for the stock market? The increase in investment incentives might be expected to result in excess returns on new investment and thereby cause firm value to rise. That view of the economy is, however, essentially static; it assumes that the increase in investment has no effects on the profitability of existing assets.

A competing, dynamic view suggests that if competition eliminated any excess return on new investment, the value of existing assets—which compete in the output markets against the new assets, but are not afforded the advantage of expensing—must decline. Because the value of the firm reflects the value of its underlying assets, firm value would decline.[6]

The effects of fundamental tax reform on firm value appear to be theoretically ambiguous and depend on the impact of those two different effects on firm value. Theoretical models of tax reform by Auerbach (1989), Gravelle (1984), Lyon (1989a), and Summers (1981, 1983) have noted the ambiguity. Where the installation of new capital incurs adjustment costs, the marginal cost of adjustment limits the expansion of new investment and provides a cushion limiting the decline in the value of existing capital. Those adjustment costs may be related to installation costs, interference with current production, and the managerial effort needed to increase the capital stock. If marginal adjustment costs increase with the amount of new investment undertaken, inframarginal new investment could earn an excess return. The change in firm value then would reflect a mixture of two effects: the decline in the value of existing assets and the excess return earned on inframarginal new investment.

Figures 3–1 and 3–2 depict the two competing views. Both figures represent the effects of a switch from a tax on true economic income to a tax system providing for the immediate expensing of new investment, and both assume a constant tax rate. Figure 3–1 shows the possible expansion of capital stock in

FIGURE 3–1

Increase in Investment Demand under Consumption Tax
without Adjustment Costs

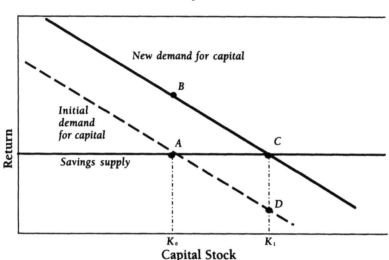

the absence of any adjustment costs to the installation of new capital. Under the income tax, equilibrium is initially at point A, corresponding to capital stock K_0. Elimination of the tax burden on new capital by the introduction of expensing initially increases the return to new capital to point B. Because that return exceeds the required return to savers, investment increases until a new equilibrium is reached at point C, corresponding to the increased capital stock K_1. Old capital purchased immediately before the switch to expensing, however, does not receive the benefit of expensing and earns the lower return corresponding to point D. To offer the same rate of return as new capital, old capital must decline in value.

Figure 3–2 repeats the analysis but includes adjustment costs. Again, the elimination of the tax burden on new capital initially increases the return to new capital, to point B. However, as the rate of investment increases, adjustment costs are posited to increase (as depicted by the curve for the marginal adjustment cost). At point C', the return on new capital less the marginal adjustment cost is just sufficient to compensate savers for the use of their funds. As a result, equilibrium is achieved with a smaller expansion of the capital stock (K'_1) than in the absence of adjustment costs. Given the smaller expansion of the capital stock, the return to old capital purchased immediately before the switch to a consumption tax decreases by a smaller amount, corresponding to point D'.

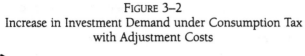

FIGURE 3–2
Increase in Investment Demand under Consumption Tax
with Adjustment Costs

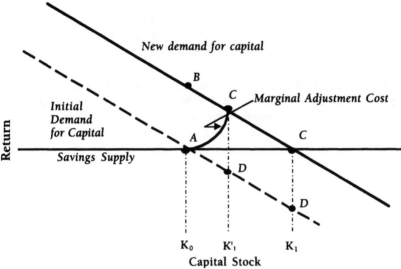

With adjustment costs, old capital must still decline in value, but by less than in the absence of adjustment costs. Further, new capital added between quantities K_0 and K'_1 earns a return slightly in excess of that needed to compensate savers for the use of their funds because on these units of investment, marginal adjustment costs are less than at K'_1. To the extent that existing firms can best undertake new investment, the excess return on new capital benefits the stockholders of existing firms.

The switch to a consumption tax also causes a potential loss of depreciation deductions on existing capital and may be accompanied by a change in the tax rates at both the corporate and individual levels. A more specific examination, provided later, considers the tax treatment of different corporate assets under the actual income tax system in the United States. We find that the transition to a consumption tax would likely result in diverse effects on asset prices because the current income tax system treats different assets unequally. Before a more precise inquiry into the theoretical effects of a transition to a consumption tax, we consider empirical evidence of the effects of tax reform on asset prices.

Empirical Evidence from Prior Tax Reforms. Empirical research on the effects of tax reform on firm value is limited. Several event studies have examined stock market returns around the dates of significant legislative events leading to changes in the tax system. The pattern of cross-sectional returns is then examined for correlation with variables supporting either the static view or the dynamic view.

Lyon (1989a) considers four separate events involving the repeal and reinstatement of the investment tax credit (ITC) in the 1960s and early 1970s. The introduction of an ITC is similar to the introduction of expensing under a consumption tax: both reforms reduce only the taxation of new investment without changing the tax treatment of existing assets. Lyon finds that the change in company stock market values correlates positively to the expected receipt of investment tax credits following the introduction of the investment tax credit; his finding supports the static view. The magnitude of the change in firm value is quantitatively and statistically significant. For each dollar of current tax savings resulting from the investment tax credit, firm value increased by several times this amount. The increase suggests that future investment was also thought to generate excess returns. Surprisingly, the study finds no evidence of a decline in value associated with existing capital. Investors in the stock market may reason that firms with existing assets are in the best position to undertake profitable new investment. Further, the investment tax credit is an offset to income tax; consequently, start-up firms might not benefit from the credit for several years due to a lack of profitability.

Downs and Tehranian (1988) examine the 1981 introduction of the accelerated cost-recovery system, which provided for rapid write-offs of equipment and structures. Their findings suggest that the act led to a reduction in stock market values (also see Feldstein 1981) and thus support the dynamic view of the economy. However, their findings are refuted in a more extensive study by Downs and Demirgures (1992), which expands the set of firms considered in the earlier study. Lyon (1989b) also finds little evidence of any effect on stock market values from this reform.

Cutler (1988) examines the introduction of the Tax Reform Act of 1986, which repealed the investment tax credit and reduced corporate and personal statutory tax rates. His most consistent finding is that firms with a high rate of investment before enactment of the reform fell in value. The drop could reflect the loss in expected receipts of the investment tax credit on future investment (a finding that supports the static view) or the reduced after-tax value of remaining depreciation deductions on prior investment resulting from the statutory rate reduction (a result that neither supports nor refutes either view). Other variables used to test the dynamic view are generally not statistically significant.[7]

In sum, the empirical evidence to date provides little support for the dynamic view that stock market values would decline following the introduction of a consumption tax. However, extrapolating from the empirical studies requires caution. Past empirical studies focus on a relatively few dates surrounding legislative action, and these tax changes were smaller in scope than a switch to a consumption tax. Further, investors in the stock market might experience difficulty in incorporating such reforms correctly into stock market values at the onset of reform. In the long run, however, if the dynamic view is correct—that earnings on existing assets would decline following the adoption of an investment tax credit— the stock market value eventually would be expected to drop as the earnings of corporations fell below forecast earnings.

The fundamental tax reforms under consideration are even more complicated than previous reforms. As shown in the next section, the introduction of a consumption tax would have a quite varied effect on the value of different kinds of assets even under a dynamic view of the economy. Some assets might increase in value while others decrease. The change in a company's total value would then require an appropriate aggregation of the change in value of each type of asset. In the economy as a whole, such an aggregation results in a significantly smaller decline in total value than suggested by prior studies based on only a single asset type, even under the extreme assumptions of the dynamic view.

Theoretical Framework. Our current income tax system is not a pure income tax. Under a Haig-Simons measure of income, any decrease in the real value of a firm's underlying assets would be deducted from income (and any increase included in income). In lieu of an attempt to determine the value of a firm's assets at each point in time, the tax code stipulates a schedule of depreciation allowances for all assets. (Certain assets, such as land, are not depreciable.) Even if the present value of the statutorily defined depreciation allowances fortuitously approximated the present value of economic depreciation, the period-by-period statutory deductions would surely not equal economic depreciation. As a result, at any point in time, the replacement cost of an asset would generally be different from its remaining value for tax purposes.

Consider an income tax system in which firms are indifferent between the purchase of a unit of capital for $1 and the retention of the dollar for other purposes. Indifference implies that the present value of the after-tax cash flows from the capital investment equals $1. For the capital investment, cash flows consist of the net after-tax revenues generated from the sale of output produced with the asset (the asset's capital services) and the value of the tax depreciation allowances that the firm is allowed to claim for purchasing the asset. Cash flows from the sale of output can be considered as related to the productive capacity of the unit of capital, while the value of the depreciation allowances reflects tax attributes provided by the tax system. As the asset ages, the value of its productive capacity declines as a function of its rate of economic depreciation, and the value of its tax attributes declines on the basis of the schedule of tax depreciation allowances provided.

Now consider a switch to a consumption tax like the flat tax proposed by House Majority Leader Dick Armey.[8] For simplicity, we consider only changes in the tax structure at the corporate level. Further, general equilibrium effects that may affect relative factor prices are ignored. The switch to the consumption tax is assumed to be unanticipated.[9] Under the consumption tax, depreciation allowances may not be claimed and are simply lost. Existing assets would not benefit from resale (which would allow the purchaser to expense the asset) because the consumption tax would tax the full sales price of the asset as income to the firm. In addition to allowing the expensing of new investment, the consumption tax would provide a lower statutory tax rate on cash flow at the corporate level. The current statutory tax rate for most corporate income is 35 percent; in this example, under the flat tax, the tax rate on cash flow would be 20 percent.

As a result of the switch to the consumption tax, three separate effects would produce the total change in the value of an existing asset: (1) the loss in future tax depreciation allowances; (2) the change in the tax rate on the capital services of the asset, with the pretax value of capital services held constant; and (3) any change in the present value of the pretax capital services provided by the asset. The latter effect might occur if competition from new investment reduced the value of output produced by the existing asset or if the discount rate used by investors to value future cash flows of the asset changed.

Quantitative Assessment of Price Effects

An evaluation of the effects of a switch from the current income tax to the flat tax should consider assets with different depreciation allowances. We consider depreciable property (equipment and structures), land, and intangible capital. In addition to the treatment of these assets under the present law, we study the treatment of equipment and structures under two alternative income tax systems providing different methods of economic depreciation (economic depreciation over the life of the asset and its first-year present-value equivalent). As a result, we consider a total of five asset types:

- *Asset 1. Equipment and structures, economic depreciation over asset life.* Under a pure income tax, depreciation allowances are equal to economic depreciation (that is, the change in asset value) at each point in time. Although no depreciable asset under the current income tax system actually receives economic depreciation, it is a useful benchmark for comparison with the tax treatment of other assets.

- *Asset 2. Equipment and structures, first-year cost-recovery system.* An immediate first-year write-off equal to the present value of economic depreciation is often viewed as providing the same investment incentives as economic depreciation taken at each point in time. Although such a first-year cost-recovery system (FYCRS) has never been enacted, it was proposed by Auerbach and Jorgenson (1980). The effect of a transition to a consumption tax differs between these two alternative methods of providing economic depreciation.

TABLE 3–1

Percentage Change in Asset Values under Switch to Consumption Taxation

Asset	Tax Treatment under Initial Income Tax System	Pretax Value of Capital Services	Immediate Decline in Pretax Value of Capital Services	Increase in Discount Rate
1. Equipment and structures	Receives economic depreciation at every point in time (pure income tax)	− 9	−20	−20
2. Equipment and structures	Receives present value of economic depreciation (first-year write-off)	+23	+8	+8
3. Equipment and structures	Actual U.S. tax system (MACRS)	See table 3–3	See table 3–4	See table 3–5
4. Land	Non depreciable	+23	−20	−20
5. Intangible capital	Expensed at time of purchase	+23	+23	+8

NOTE: For assets 1, 2, and 5, where it is necessary to make additional assumptions, a rate of economic depreciation of 0.15 and a real discount rate of 5.0 percent are assumed.

• *Asset 3. Equipment and structures, modified accelerated cost-recovery system (MACROS) (present law).* Under present law, for regular tax purposes, equipment is generally recovered over 3, 5, 7, or 10 years under the 200 percent declining balance method switching to straight line. Certain public utility property is recovered over 15 and 20 years under the 150 percent declining balance method switching to straight line. Residential rental property and nonresidential structures are recovered by the straight-line method over periods of 27.5 and 39 years, respectively.[10]

• *Asset 4. Land.* Land is not depreciated over time under the income tax. Land would be expensed under the flat tax.

• *Asset 5. Intangible capital.* Costs of creating intangible capital are expensed under the current income tax even though these assets may have lasting value.[11] Intangible capital would also be expensed under the flat tax.

The first column of table 3–1 summarizes the tax treatment of different assets under the income tax.

For each of these five asset types, we consider separately the change in value resulting from (1) the loss in future tax depreciation allowances; (2) the change in the tax rate on the capital services of the asset, with the pretax value of capital services held constant; and (3) any change in the present value of the pretax capital services provided by the asset. For the latter change, we consider alternative adjustment processes ranging from unchanged pretax value of capital services (static) to a decline commensurate with an immediate expansion of the capital stock to its long-run equilibrium value (dynamic).

Change in Asset Values from Loss of Depreciation Allowances. Following the switch to a consumption tax, the loss of future depreciation allowances affects differently the five assets considered above. Only asset 1 (assets receiving economic depreciation at each point in time) and potentially asset 3 (assets depreciated under the modified accelerated cost-recovery system) have any remaining depreciation allowances under the income tax. These two assets are examined in turn.

• *Assets 1 and 2. Equipment and structures, economic depreciation.* Even though, under the income tax, both assets 1 and 2 receive depreciation allowances equal in present value to economic depreciation, the switch to the consumption tax would cause only asset 1 to lose future depreciation allowances. With the after-tax value of capital services held constant for the moment, the loss in future depreciation allowances would cause asset 1 to decline in percentage terms by the after-tax present value of remaining depreciation allowances.

For most equipment, the present value of economic depreciation ranges between 0.60 and 0.90 per dollar of asset value.[12] For longer-lived structures, the present value of economic depreciation may be less than 0.40. At a 35 percent statutory income tax, the percentage change in value from the loss in depreciation allowances would range from less than 14 percent for structures to as much as 32 percent for quickly depreciating equipment. Without any other change in the after-tax present value of capital services, the loss in depreciation allowances would be the only effect on the value of asset 1.

• *Asset 3. Equipment and structures, modified accelerated cost-recovery system.* Under the existing U.S. tax system, the depreciation of equipment and structures has characteristics that are a blend of the treatments of assets 1 and 2. As for asset 1, depreciation deductions for equipment and structures are taken ratably over time.[13] But as for asset 2, depreciation deductions for most equip-

TABLE 3–2
Percentage Change in Asset Value from Loss of Depreciation Allowances
for Three-Year, Five-Year, and Seven-Year Equipment

Years of Depreciation Allowances Claimed before Loss in Future Deductions	Three-Year Asset	Five-Year Asset	Seven-Year Asset
0.5 year	-28	-28	-27
1.5 years	-16	-21	-22
2.5 years	- 8	-15	-18
3.5 years	0	-11	-14
4.5 years	0	- 4	-11
5.5 years	0	0	- 8
6.5 years	0	0	- 3
7.5 years or more	0	0	0

NOTE: The percentage change in asset value is calculated as $-uR_t/[1-\mu(Z-R_t)]$, where u is the statutory corporate income tax rate, Z is the present value of tax depreciation allowances on one dollar of new capital (before replacement of the income tax with the consumption tax), and R_t is the remaining present value of tax depreciation on an asset purchased t years ago that has a current replacement cost of one dollar. R_t is calculated as $Z_t[(1-\delta)(1+\pi)]-t$, where Z_t is the present value of remaining depreciation allowances on an asset purchased for one dollar t years ago, δ is the annual rate of economic depreciation, and π is the annual inflation rate. In these calculations, the assumed rates of economic depreciation are 0.3125, 0.1316 and 0.0833 for assets in the three-year, five-year, and seven-year classes, respectively. The assumed annual rate of inflation is 3.5 percent, and the real annual discount rate is assumed to be 5.0 percent, with a nominal discount rate of approximately 8.7 percent. Depreciation allowances are calculated with the 200 percent declining balance method with a switch to straight line and incorporate the half-year convention.

ment are accelerated relative to economic depreciation, and there is a point in time when an asset is fully depreciated and no further depreciation deductions may be taken. As a result, assets with accelerated depreciation deductions derive a decreasing percentage of value over time from the value of future depreciation deductions. For fully depreciated assets, no value is attributable to future depreciation deductions.

Table 3–2 shows the percentage decline in asset value from the loss of depreciation allowances for various types of equipment depreciated over three years, five years, and seven years under the U.S. income tax. For example, for an asset such as a tractor truck cab, which is recovered over three years, the loss in depreciation allowances after one-half year of depreciation has been claimed causes a 28 percent decline in value of the asset. However, the loss in depreciation allowances after two and one-half years results in only an 8 percent decline in value. The asset is fully depreciated after three and one-half years; a switch to a consumption tax after that date would cause no decline in value through the loss in depreciation allowances. Table 3–2 shows similar patterns in the decline in asset value from the loss of depreciation allowances for representative five-year and seven-year assets.[14]

Total Change in Asset Values from Consumption Taxation: Three Cases. In addition to the change in asset values from the loss of tax depreciation allowances, two other effects must be assessed to measure the overall impact on asset values: (1) the effect of any change in the statutory tax rate on the capital services of the asset, with the pretax value of capital services held constant, and (2) any change in the present value of the pretax capital services provided by the asset. As discussed earlier, the latter effect can arise if the consumption tax changes the overall level of desired investment in the economy.

In this section, we consider three different adjustment processes for the pretax value of capital services. In the *first* case, the pretax value of capital services is held constant when a flat tax replaces the income tax. Such an extreme case, though unlikely, could occur at least theoretically if adjustment costs strictly limited the amount of new investment that could be undertaken.[15] This is the static view.

In the *second* case, the pretax value of capital services from existing capital would fall to the value that would apply to new investment in the absence of adjustment costs. Under this scenario, the price of capital services would be flexible, and new and old investments would be perfect substitutes. This is the dynamic view.

The *third* case is based on Gravelle 1995, which suggests that, in the short run, the value of the capital services provided by existing assets might not change, but the real after-tax discount rate at which firms value future capital services might be bid up by the expanded demand for capital. That assumption is consistent with a fixed short-run supply of savings. In an open economy, however, even in the short run, funds for new investment might be

TABLE 3–3

Percentage Change in Asset Value under Switch to Consumption Tax
without Change in Pretax Value of Capital Services for
Three-Year, Five-Year, and Seven-Year Equipment

Years of Depreciation Allowances Claimed before Switch	Three-Year Asset	Five-Year Asset	Seven-Year Asset
0.5 year	-12	-11	-10
1.5 years	4	- 2	- 4
2.5 years	13	5	1
3.5 years	23	10	6
4.5 years	23	18	9
5.5 years	23	23	13
6.5 years	23	23	19
7.5 years or more	23	23	23

NOTE: The percentage change in asset value is calculated as:

$$\frac{\frac{(u-\tau)(1-uZ)}{1-u} - uR_t}{1-uZ+uR_t}$$

where u is the statutory corporate income tax rate, τ is the consumption tax rate, Z is the present value of tax depreciation allowances on one dollar of new capital (before replacement of the income tax with the consumption tax), and R_t is the present value of remaining tax depreciation on an asset purchased t years ago that has a current replacement cost of one dollar. See the note to table 3-2 for the derivation of R_t. In these calculations, $u=.35$ and $\tau=.20$.

expected to be quite elastic. That situation has been convincingly demonstrated in the United States during the past two decades. Due to large federal budget deficits, national savings were very low, yet investment remained strong. In any case, if one assumes a fixed supply of savings and a close relationship between domestic savings and domestic investment (see, for example, Feldstein and Horioka 1980), tax reform would cause the pretax value of all components of firm value—including existing assets, monopoly rents, and intangibles—to decline, regardless of the degree of competitiveness faced by the sector in which the firm operated.

The three alternative cases are intended to help bracket the potential range of effects on asset prices. Each scenario is an extreme representation of the changes most likely to occur.

Case 1. Pretax value of capital services held constant. First, the effect of fundamental tax reform on asset values is analyzed with the pretax value of capital services held constant. This case can be considered the static response to a change to a consumption tax. The example assumes that the value of the pretax marginal product of existing capital would not change, nor would the discount rate used to evaluate future cash flows from these assets. The relative price level is also assumed to be unaffected by a switch to a consumption tax. The changes in valuation would occur through two effects: (1) the loss in value of depreciation tax deductions and (2) the difference in the rate of taxation.

The net change in the value of an asset consists of the increase in value from the reduced taxation of the capital services (given that the statutory tax rate under the consumption tax is less than the statutory tax rate on corporate income), less the decline in value from the loss of future depreciation allowances on this asset discussed in the previous section.

The second column of table 3–1 shows the percentage change in asset value from a switch to consumption taxation for four of the five general types of assets considered initially, with the pretax value of capital services held constant. Table 3–3 provides the details for asset 3 (assets depreciated under the actual MACRS rules). All calculations assume a consumption tax rate of 20 percent and a corporate income tax rate of 35 percent. For asset 1 the present value of economic depreciation per dollar of investment is assumed to be 0.75.

Asset 1 would decrease in value by 9 percent (see column 3 of table 3–1). The decline in value is a function of the asset's true rate of economic depreciation. For long-lived assets (assets with a present value of economic depreciation less than 0.535), the change in value could be positive. For more typical equipment assets (assets with a present value of economic depreciation ranging between 0.60 and 0.90), the net decline in the value of asset 1 would be 3–16 percent. The values for assets 2, 4, and 5 would increase by 23 percent from the switch to consumption taxation—assuming there were no change in the pretax value of their capital services (see column 3 of table 3–1). The situation would be the same for the increase in the value of intangible assets, which would occur because of a 23 percent increase in the after-tax rate of return when the tax rate on cash flow was reduced from 35 percent to 20 percent.

For asset 3, the magnitude and direction of the change in asset value would depend on the present value of remaining depreciation allowances, which would vary with the asset's vintage and MACRS recovery period. Table 3–3 shows the percentage change in value for equipment of different vintages depreciated over three, five, and seven years under the actual income tax system. For assets recently purchased, the decline in value from the loss of future depreciation deductions would be greater than the increase in value from the lower rate of taxation. For example, for an asset depreciated over three years, a switch to the 20 percent flat tax after only one-half year's worth of depreciation had been claimed would result in a 12 percent decline in the value of the asset. However, after two and one-half years' of depreciation had been claimed, the representative equipment shown for the three-year, five-year, and seven-year depreciation classes would all increase in value by switching to the consumption tax. Assets that were already completely recovered would experience a 23 percent increase in value, the same as shown for assets 2, 4, and 5 in column 3 of table 3–1.

Case 2. Decline in pretax value of capital services, discount rates held constant. The changes in asset value considered so far hold the pretax value of capital services constant when the flat tax replaces the current income tax. In general, however, one would expect increased investment under the flat tax because the reduced rate of taxation would allow additional investment—that would not have been profitable under the income tax—to be undertaken.

An increase in the capital stock would lower the pretax value of the capital services on marginal new investment. Because existing investment competes to some extent against new investment, the pretax value of the capital services on existing investment should also decline, at least in part. The decline in the value of the capital services on existing capital would completely reflect the lower value of the capital services on new investment if new investment and old investment were perfect substitutes. For many assets, this substitution might be possible. However, new investment may not be a direct substitute for other assets, as illustrated by the case of a Stradivarius. Similarly, some investments using nonreplicable intangible inputs might not face direct competition from new investment.

To contrast with the earlier static assumption, this section assumes that the pretax value of capital services on existing assets would decline such that the after-tax return on a new asset would be the same before and after the reform (the dynamic case). It is also assumed that the switch to consumption taxation would not affect the purchase price of new investment goods, and after-tax discount rates would remain constant.

Under these assumptions, the fourth column of table 3–1 shows the change in value for four of the five general types of assets. Table 3–4 details asset 3 (assets depreciated under the actual MACRS rules).

TABLE 3–4
Percentage Change in Asset Value under Switch to 20 Percent
Consumption Tax with Immediate Decline in
Pretax Value of Capital Services for
Three-Year, Five-Year, and Seven-Year Equipment

Years of Depreciation Allowances Claimed before Switch	Three-Year Asset	Five-Year Asset	Seven-Year Asset
0.5 year	-15	-17	-18
1.5 years	0	- 9	-13
2.5 years	9	- 2	- 8
3.5 years	18	2	- 4
4.5 years	18	10	0
5.5 years	18	15	3
6.5 years	18	15	9
7.5 years or more	18	15	12

NOTE: The pretax value of capital services is assumed to decline sufficiently so that the after-tax value of capital services is equal to $1-\tau$, where τ is the tax rate on cash flow under the consumption tax. Together with the tax deduction of τ on a $1 investment in new capital, this is equal to the purchase cost of the investment. The statutory corporate income tax rate is u and the present value of tax depreciation allowances on one dollar of new capital is Z. The percentage change in asset value is calculated as

$$\frac{-\tau + uZ - uR_t}{1 - uZ + uR_t}$$

See the note to table 3-2 for the derivation of R_t. In these calculations, $u=.35$ and $\tau=.20$.

• *Asset 1. Equipment and structures, economic depreciation over asset life.* The net decline in asset value would be 20 percent. The decline in value, which is independent of the asset's true rate of economic depreciation, would be a greater decline than under the case 1 assumption of no change in the pretax value of capital services.

• *Asset 2. Equipment and structures, first-year cost-recovery system.* Although the expansion of the capital stock would reduce the value of the flow of capital services for the asset in the same manner as for asset 1, asset 2 would suffer no additional loss in value because no remaining depreciation deductions would be claimed. For typical equipment assets, the value of the asset would still increase, but by less than in the static case. Given a representative equipment asset, the asset value would increase by 8 percent. In this case, the reduced rate at which the cash flows from existing assets were taxed would offset the decline in the pretax value of capital services as investment expands.

• *Asset 3. Equipment and structures, modified accelerated cost-recovery system.* Assets not fully depreciated would lose future depreciation allowances. Additionally, asset 3 would experience a similar change in value from the flow of capital services as for assets 1 and 2.

Table 3–4 shows the change in value from a switch to a 20 percent consumption tax for equipment of different vintages depreciated over three, five, and seven years under the current income tax. Relative to table 3–3, which assumes that the pretax value of capital services did not change, the decline in asset value would be greater (increase in asset value is smaller). For example, a five-year asset on which only one-half year's depreciation allowance had been claimed would be expected to decline in value by 17 percent. The decline would contrast with only an 11 percent decline in the static case. Fully depreciated assets would increase in value by less than in the static case. A fully depreciated five-year asset would increase in value by 15 percent in a switch to a consumption tax, relative to an increase of 23 percent in the static case. The increase in value would be positively related to the present value of depreciation allowances under the initial income tax.

• *Asset 4. Land.* The change in value of asset 4 (column 3 of table 3–1) would be the same as for asset 1—a 20 percent decline. For land, the loss in value would result entirely from a decline in the pretax value of its capital services because there would be no loss of depreciation allowances.

• *Asset 5. Intangible capital.* The change in value of asset 5 in the dynamic case (column 4 of table 3–1) would be identical to the static case (column 3 of table 3–1). Intangible capital is expensed under the income tax and would likewise be expensed under the consumption tax. As a result, intangible investment would not increase under the consumption tax. Existing intangible assets, however, would benefit from the decline in the statutory tax rate applying to the cash flows generated by these assets. Under the existing tax system, those cash flows would be taxed at 35 percent, but under the consumption tax, they would be taxed at only 20 percent. The increase in value of intangible capital would be 23 percent.

TABLE 3–5
Percentage Change in Asset Value under Switch to Consumption Tax
with Increase in Discount Rate for
Three-Year, Five-Year, and Seven-Year Equipment

Years of Depreciation Allowances Claimed before Switch	Three-Year Asset	Five-Year Asset	Seven-Year Asset
0.5 year	-18	-23	-25
1.5 years	- 3	-15	-20
2.5 years	5	- 9	-16
3.5 years	15	- 5	-12
4.5 years	15	2	- 9
5.5 years	15	7	- 6
6.5 years	15	7	- 1
7.5 years or more	15	7	2

NOTE: The percentage change in asset value is calculated as

$$\frac{\dfrac{1-\tau}{1-u}\left[\dfrac{r+\delta}{\dfrac{r}{1-u}+\delta}\right](1-uZ)}{1-uZ+uR_t}-1$$

In these calculations, $u = .35$, $\tau = .20$, and $r = .05$. See table 3-2 for assumptions on δ, Z, and R_t.

Case 3. Physical capital services held constant, increase in discount rate. As in Gravelle's 1995 analysis, the marginal product of capital would be unchanged by the switch to the consumption tax, but the real after-tax discount rate would increase. In that extreme case, savings would be fixed in supply: consequently, the increase in demand for investment would affect only the rate of interest. The increase in the discount rate would be sufficient so that an investor under the consumption tax would be indifferent to undertaking new investment for assets that formerly received tax depreciation equal to economic depreciation. For such an asset, the discount rate must increase by 54 percent, given a 35 percent statutory tax rate under the income tax. The percentage change in value is shown in the fifth column of table 3–1 for four of the five asset types. Table 3–5 presents additional details for asset 3 (assets assumed to be depreciated under the MACRS rules).

• *Asset 1. Equipment and structures, economic depreciation over asset life.* The percentage reduction in value would be 20 percent. The decline in value would be the same as under the assumption that the marginal product of capital declined.

• *Asset 2. Equipment and structures, first-year cost-recovery system.* The percentage change in value would also be the same as under the case 2 assumption. For a representative equipment asset, the value would increase by 8 percent.

• *Asset 3. Equipment and structure, modified accelerated cost-recovery system.* The percentage change in value would depend on the asset's vintage and MACRS class, because these factors affect the present value of unclaimed depreciation allowances. For assets claiming future tax depreciation allowances that in present value exceed economic depreciation, the decline in value could exceed 20 percent. For older assets, a lesser amount of depreciation benefits would be lost by the switch to the consumption tax, and the decline in value would be less, or the asset might even increase in value.

Table 3–5 shows the change in values for assets depreciated over three years, five years, and seven years under the current income tax system. As shown for five-year and seven-year assets that have only one-half year of depreciation allowances already claimed, the decline in value would be greater than 20 percent. For fully recovered assets, the value of all assets shown would increase.

• *Asset 4. Land.* Like asset 1, the percentage reduction in the value of land would be 20 percent, the same result as under the case 2 assumption.

• *Asset 5. Intangible capital.* The increase in discount rates would affect intangible capital differently from the case 2 assumption. Recall that intangible capital is expensed under the income tax. If discount rates increased but the marginal product of intangible capital did not change, new investment in intangible capital would no longer be profitable under the consumption tax. For existing assets, the higher discount rate would tend to reduce the value of the asset, but the lower consumption tax rate would tend to increase its value. Which effect would be greater would depend on the rate of economic depreciation of the intangible capital. For a quickly depreciating asset, the change in discount rates would have a relatively slight effect on the value of the asset, and the change in the tax rate would be dominant. For a representative intangible asset with a present value of economic depreciation of 0.75, the asset value would increase by 8 percent (column 5 of table 3–1), the same as for asset 2.

Other Transitional Issues

In addition to effects on asset price, fundamental tax reform might cause shareholder wealth to change through other channels. Moreover, if tax reform were anticipated, taxpayers could be expected to engage in a variety of tax arbitrage activities.

Debt. Replacing the income tax with a flat tax could have very different effects on debt and equity holders than a retail sales tax would. Consider first short-term debt. Changes in the interest rate would not generally affect the nominal value of that debt. As noted by Gravelle (1995), given no change in the overall price level and with the absence of bankruptcy risk, shareholders alone would have to bear the change in asset values caused by implementation of the flat tax.[16] By contrast, under a consumption tax that was fully passed through to consumers, bondholders would bear a portion of the change in the real value of assets through a decline in real purchasing power.

Under all proposals for a consumption tax, interest expense would no longer be deductible at the business level.[17] In the Modigliani and Miller (1963) model, the ability to deduct interest expense under present law increases the value of the firm; consequently, the elimination of interest deductibility would decrease the value of equity. The magnitude of the effect would depend on how interest rates adjusted. That adjustment would depend on changes in the taxation of individuals as well as corporations.

Entity Tax Attributes. All recent proposals for tax reform would eliminate tax attributes, such as net operating loss carryforwards, and various credit carryforwards, such as AMT credits, and would thereby reduce the market value of a firm possessing these attributes.

Fixed Price Contracts; Regulated Industries. Wealth effects may arise from fundamental tax reform as a result of inflexible prices fixed by contract or regulatory bodies. Examples include employee compensation packages and utility rates.

Because prices might not be able to adjust quickly, the wealth effects arising from the imposition of a consumption tax might depend on whether the buyer or seller was the object of taxation (regardless of which party had the obligation to collect tax). For example, unlike the typical value-added tax or retail sales tax, a subtraction-method VAT (such as the USA business tax) would be drafted as a direct tax; under such a law, the object of taxation would be the seller. Consequently, absent transitional rules, the unanticipated imposition of a subtraction method VAT might cause a windfall loss to the selling party in a fixed-price supply contract (and a windfall gain to the buying party). Similarly, the imposition of a subtraction method VAT would likely cause a windfall loss to regulated utility company shareholders because of lags in the rate-making process.

As another example, the flat tax would impose tax on certain employer-provided fringe benefits by denying a deduction to the employer. Under standard incidence assumptions, employees would carry the burden of such a tax as if the employees had paid the tax directly. However, because employers often have limited flexibility to adjust compensation packages, a portion of the tax on fringe benefits would likely fall on shareholders. In the case of employee health benefits, numerous employers have committed to providing benefits to employees during their retirement years. Replacing the income tax with the flat tax or a retail sales tax would increase the after-tax cost of providing such a benefit, and current shareholders would likely bear that additional cost through lower share values.

Accounting Methods. Under present law, most large businesses are required to use the accrual method of accounting for tax purposes. Absent transitional relief, replacing an accrual-based income tax with a cash-based consumption tax, such as the flat tax, would cause accrued but unreceived income to be taxed twice and accrued but unpaid expense to be deducted twice. Similarly, paid but unaccrued expenses would never be deducted, and received but unaccrued income would never be included in the tax base. To the extent that accounts receivable exceeded accounts payable, the adoption of a cash-method consumption tax, without transition rules, would inflict a windfall loss to shareholders.

Shareholder Issues. Most proposals for fundamental tax reform would change the taxation of shareholders and bondholders in addition to the previously considered taxation of business entities. Thus, transitional wealth effects would arise from changes in income taxes for both the individual and the corporation. For example, a decline in the value of corporate equity due to the introduction of a flat tax might be offset—if the equity were held in a qualified pension plan—by a reduction in the tax rate applicable to pension withdrawals under the individual income tax.

Even without any change in shareholder taxation, the transitional wealth effects associated with fundamental tax reform might not affect all shareholders alike. As noted by Grubert and Newlon (1995), the imposition of a consumption tax that was passed through to final consumers as higher U.S. prices would not affect foreign shareholders (and U.S. emigrants) who consumed their wealth outside the United States. Under a consumption tax that is passed forward to consumers, any transition rule designed to mitigate the windfall losses of domestic shareholders from the repeal of the income tax would create windfall gains for foreign shareholders.

Tax Arbitrage. In the United States, unlike some countries with parliamentary forms of government, taxpayers typically have many months' notice from the first consideration of tax changes until the enactment of such legislation. Tax legislation requires the support of both houses in Congress as well as the president, and the political parties have frequently divided control over these institutions. As a result of legislative lags and of a reluctance to enact retroactive tax changes, taxpayers generally have some opportunity to prepare for pending tax changes. We use the term *tax arbitrage* to refer to transition-induced changes in the timing or characterization of transactions.

Anticipated changes in tax rates and tax preferences often motivate tax arbitrage transactions. For example, an anticipated increase in tax rates would encourage the acceleration of income and the deferral of expense, while an anticipated decline in tax rates would encourage the deferral of income and the acceleration of expense. Similarly, the anticipated elimination of an investment tax credit might accelerate investment, while the anticipated enactment of a new credit might cause investment activity to be deferred. Fundamental tax reform would create similar opportunities for tax arbitrage, although the form of the consumption tax would likely affect the type of tax arbitrage.

Adoption of a consumption tax that was passed forward to consumers as higher prices would create an incentive for consumers to accelerate purchases of goods that could be stored at a cost less than the tax. (If the consumption tax were imposed on payment rather than on delivery, there also would be an incentive to prepay for goods and services for future delivery.) Bull and Lindsey (1995) point out the macroeconomic implications of anticipatory consumer purchases. Such a consumption tax would create no similar incentive for businesses to accelerate purchases because the relative prices of outputs and inputs, after tax, would not be affected.

By contrast, a consumption tax that was not passed forward as higher consumer prices would not create incentives for consumers to accelerate purchases of storable goods. For example, under the usual incidence assumptions, the anticipated introduction of a flat tax would not, by itself, stimulate consumer sales. Absent transitional relief, however, such a tax would in many cases create an incentive for businesses to defer the purchase of depreciable, amortizable, and inventory property until after the effective date. Business purchases made after the effective date would be immediately and fully deductible; in contrast, the cost of business purchases made before the effective date might not be fully recovered. Thus, under conventional incidence assumptions, the anticipated introduction of a flat tax could temporarily depress the economy, but the anticipated introduction of a VAT or retail sales tax could cause a transitory economic boom.

Policy Responses to Transition

With the notable exception of the USA tax, none of the recent legislative proposals to restructure the federal tax system have included rules to mitigate changes in asset value. Although the USA tax transition rules generally pro-

TABLE 3–6
Amortization under USA Tax

Asset	Transitional Basis Amortization Period
Remaining depreciation, with amortization period less than 15 years	10 years
Remaining depreciation, with amortization period greater than or equal to 15 years	30 years
Inventory property	3 years
Other property (including land)	40 years

vide no recovery for income tax attributes (for example, net operating losses, income tax credits, alternative minimum tax credits, passive losses), the income tax basis in assets acquired before the effective date would be recoverable if the purchase of these assets would have been deductible under the general USA tax rules. The adjusted tax basis in those assets would be recovered over one of four amortization periods, as shown in table 3–6 (see section 290 of S. 722). Other alternatives for transition include the write-off of basis in existing assets under the current law's rules for capital cost recovery (see, for example, Hall and Rabushka 1995, 116) or the allowance of an immediate deduction for unrecovered basis in assets.

Transitional Basis Recovery under a Flat Tax. Perhaps the most persuasive argument for transitional relief is to eliminate large unanticipated changes in taxpayer wealth (see Graetz 1985). Thus, one way to judge various transition rules is to measure their effectiveness in reducing changes in wealth.

This section considers two transition rules. The first transition rule would allow asset owners to deduct the unrecovered basis of the asset against cash flow immediately or receive the equivalent of this amount in present value. The second transition rule would allow depreciation on existing assets to continue, but deductions would be taken at the new tax rate.

• *Asset 1. Equipment and structures, economic depreciation over asset life.* Assets receiving economic depreciation at each point in time would benefit under either transition rule. If basis were to be recovered immediately, asset values would increase by twenty percentage points relative to the values calculated earlier (columns 2–4 of table 3–1). If, alternatively, depreciation were allowed to continue, asset values would increase by thirteen to fifteen percentage points relative to the value wtive equipment asset.

In the static case (column 2 of table 3–1) without transition relief, continuing economic depreciation would result in an unambiguous net increase in value for all assets, independent of their rate of economic depreciation. In that case, allowing depreciation to continue would be more generous than necessary to avoid wealth changes. In the dynamic cases, columns 3 and 4 of table 3–1 without transition relief, immediate write-off of basis would be necessary to avoid wealth changes.

• *Asset 2. Equipment and structures, first-year cost-recovery system.* These would not receive any benefit from these two transition rules because such assets would have been already fully depreciated for tax purposes before the transition to the consumption tax.

• *Asset 3. Equipment and structures, modified accelerated cost-recovery system.* Because actual depreciation schedules do not exactly follow economic depreciation, the transition rules would have a more varied effect on assets of different vintages.

Tables 3–7 through 3–9 show the effects of the transition rules under the three different equilibrium assumptions (case 1, no change in value of capital services; case 2, decline in marginal product; case 3, increase in discount rate) for three-, five-, and seven-year assets. In the static case (case 1), shown in table 3–7, continuing depreciation would be too generous for all vintages and would result in an increase in the value of all assets. (As seen in table 3–3, without transition relief only the value of assets purchased within the past one or two years might decline.)

In the dynamic cases (cases 2 and 3), continuing depreciation would not always be sufficient to prevent any decline in wealth from the transition to the flat tax. As shown in table 3–8, five-year and seven-year assets that have received only one-half year's depreciation deduction before the switch to the flat tax would still experience a slight decline in value. Allowing an immediate write-off of remaining basis would be sufficient to prevent a decline in wealth from the transition to the flat tax as shown in table 3–8 for assets in the three-year, five-year, and seven-year depreciation classes.

Obviously, the immediate write-off of remaining basis would be more advantageous than continuing depreciation on assets with remaining basis. The difference between these two transition rules would not be great, however, for these assets. More surprising perhaps, neither allowing an immediate deduction for remaining basis nor permitting continued depreciation would equalize the changes in asset prices across vintages (and across asset classes). In all cases, fully depreciated assets would be treated more favorably than assets with remaining basis at the time of the switch to the consumption tax. While the two transition rules considered would not equalize changes in asset values across vintages, they would reduce the variation in wealth effects across vintages.[18]

TABLE 3–7

Transition Relief and
Percentage Change in Asset Value under Switch to Consumption Tax
without Change in Pretax Value of Capital Services for
Three-Year, Five-Year, and Seven-Year Equipment

Years of Depreciation Allowances Claimed before Switch	Three-Year Asset		Five-Year Asset		Seven-Year Asset	
	Basis write-off	Continued deprecia-tion	Basis write-off	Continued deprecia-tion	Basis write-off	Continued deprecia-tion
0.5 year	5	4	6	5	8	5
1.5 years	13	13	11	9	11	9
2.5 years	18	18	14	13	13	11
3.5 years	23	23	16	16	15	14
4.5 years	23	23	20	20	16	16
5.5 years	23	23	23	23	18	18
6.5 years	23	23	23	23	21	21
7.5 years or more	23	23	23	23	23	23

NOTE: The percentage change in asset value before transition relief is calculated as in table 3–3. The transition relief of basis write-off and continued depreciation provides additional benefits of

$$\frac{\tau B_t}{1 - uZ + uR_t} \quad \text{and} \quad \frac{\tau R_t}{1 - uZ + uR_t},$$

respectively, where B_t is the remaining basis and R_t is the present value of remaining tax depreciation on an asset purchased t years ago that has a current replacement cost of one dollar. See table 3–3 for an explanation of the other variables. In these calculations, $u = .35$ and $\tau = .20$.

The effects of these transition policies would depend primarily on the process of market adjustment. If tax reform did not reduce the pretax value of capital services from existing capital, both transition policies would tend to overcorrect declines in asset value and to increase windfall gains for the types of assets shown in table 3–7. By contrast, if the pretax value of capital services declined as a result of an increase in the discount rate, both transition policies would tend to undercorrect windfall losses for recently purchased assets, as shown in table 3–9.

• *Asset 4. Land.* Land would receive a benefit equal to the deduction for its original acquisition cost if remaining basis could be written off, but would receive no benefit if depreciation were permitted to continue because land is not a depreciable asset. In the dynamic cases, where landowners experienced a decline in wealth, immediate write-off of basis would still result in a net decline in wealth unless the owner's basis in land were indexed for inflation from the date of acquisition.

• *Asset 5. Intangible capital.* Intangible assets would likewise receive no benefit under the transition rules because these assets would have no remaining basis for tax purposes.

In summary, if all assets received economic depreciation under present law and if the value of capital services from existing assets adjusted immediately to a postreform equilibrium level, then effects on asset prices would be neutralized by allowing immediate write-off of unrecovered basis. Such a policy might overcorrect declines in asset value, however, where assets received accelerated cost recovery under present law or where the value of capital services did not immediately adjust to the postreform equilibrium. No transition rule for basis recovery addresses the windfall gains that would arise from a reduction in the tax rate for assets that had been fully depreciated under present law.

Transition Relief under a Retail Sales Tax. If a retail sales tax or a VAT replaced the income tax, a firm's creditors as well as its owner would bear a portion of the change in asset values as result of an increase in the overall price level.

Transitional relief for creditors, if offered, would almost certainly need to be provided at the individual level and could be accomplished through a credit equal to the market value of debt claims at the date of transition multiplied by the (tax-inclusive) sales tax rate (assuming that the tax was fully passed through in prices). In theory, the transition relief provided at the corporate level should be reduced to the extent that creditors carried the burden of the transition. Reducing the amount of basis available for recovery by the amount of outstanding debt could achieve that result.

As discussed in "Other Transitional Issues," foreign shareholders would avoid the wealth loss caused by a rise in U.S. prices. Transitional relief provided at the corporate level would unavoidably provide equal relief to domes-

TABLE 3–8
Transition Relief and
Percentage Change in Asset Value under Switch to Consumption Tax
Assuming Immediate Decline in Pretax Value of Capital Services for
Three-Year, Five-Year, and Seven-Year Equipment

Years of Depreciation Allowances Already Claimed before Switch	Three-Year Asset		Five-Year Asset		Seven-Year Asset	
	Basis write-off	Continued deprecia-tion	Basis write-off	Continued deprecia-tion	Basis write-off	Continued deprecia-tion
0.5 year	2	1	0	- 1	0	- 3
1.5 years	9	9	4	3	2	0
2.5 years	13	13	7	6	4	2
3.5 years	18	18	9	9	5	4
4.5 years	18	18	12	12	6	6
5.5 years	18	18	15	15	8	8
6.5 years	18	18	15	15	10	10
7.5 years or more	18	18	15	15	12	12

NOTE: The percentage change in asset value before transition relief is calculated as in table 3–4. The transition relief of basis write-off and continued depreciation provides additional benefits of

$$\frac{\tau B_t}{1-uZ + uR_t} \quad \text{and} \quad \frac{\tau R_t}{1-uZ + uR_t},$$

respectively, where B_t is the remaining basis and R_t is the present value of remaining tax depreciation on an asset purchased t years ago that has a current replacement cost of one dollar. See table 3–4 for an explanation of the other variables. In these calculations, $u = .35$ and $\tau = .20$.

TABLE 3–9

Transition Relief and
Percentage Change in Asset Value under Switch to Consumption Tax
with Increase in Discount Rate for
Three-Year, Five-Year, and Seven-Year Equipment

Years of Depreciation Allowances Claimed before Switch	Three-Year Asset		Five-Year Asset		Seven-Year Asset	
	Basis write-off	Continued deprecia-tion	Basis write-off	Continued deprecia-tion	Basis write-off	Continued deprecia-tion
0.5 year	- 1	- 2	-5	-7	-7	-10
1.5 years	6	5	-2	-3	-6	- 8
2.5 years	10	10	0	-1	-4	- 6
3.5 years	15	15	2	2	-3	- 4
4.5 years	15	15	5	5	-2	- 3
5.5 years	15	15	7	7	-1	1
6.5 years	15	15	7	7	1	1
7.5 years or more	15	15	7	7	2	2

NOTE: The percentage change in asset value before transition relief is calculated as in table 3–5. The transition relief of basis write-off and continued depreciation provides additional benefits of

$$\frac{\tau B_t}{1 - uZ + uR_t} \quad \text{and} \quad \frac{\tau R'_t}{1 - uZ + uR_t},$$

respectively, where B_t is the remaining basis, and R_t and R'_t are the present values of the remaining tax depreciation on an asset purchased t years ago that has a current replacement cost of one dollar calculated at the original and new nominal discount rates, respectively. See table 3–4 for an explanation of the other variables. In these calculations, $u = .35$ and $\tau = .20$.

tic and foreign shareholders even though the wealth effects would be greater for domestic shareholders. However, if transitional relief were provided at the shareholder level, rather than at the corporate level, through a credit equal to the sales tax rate times the value of equity, shareholders would in many cases be overcompensated (see tables 3–3 through 3–5).

Tax Arbitrage. Although the case for providing transitional basis recovery to address concerns about fairness may be mixed, the failure to eliminate the effects on asset values would result in tax arbitrage activity if tax reform were anticipated. Tax arbitrage could be addressed through the retroactive imposition of tax or economically equivalent policies. For example, the incentive to defer investment pending legislative action of a flat tax could be reduced by allowing the expensing of remaining basis upon enactment of the flat tax for property acquired after the date that tax reform can reasonably be anticipated (such as the date of the tax committee's markup). (Previous enactments of the investment tax credit provide a precedent for this type of approach.)

Conclusions

Recent analyses of proposals for fundamental tax reform have suggested that major effects of asset prices would occur absent transitional relief. For example, Gravelle (1995) states, "If the flat tax rate is about 20 percent, the stock market should fall about 30 percent."

Our analysis of the transitional effects on asset prices suggests that they would not be nearly as great. For assets that benefit from accelerated depreciation under present law (as compared with a standard of economic depreciation), the benefits of a tax rate reduction would offset, at least to some extent, the loss in the ability to recover remaining basis when the income tax was replaced—particularly for many intangible assets (because the costs of creating such assets have frequently been deducted as current period expenses). Based on current market valuations (which themselves may already incorporate some probability of consumption tax reform), a significant portion of firm value appears to be attributable to intangible capital and growth opportunities.

The potential loss of other tax attributes of a firm, such as net operating losses and credit carryforwards, would result in greater declines in firm value than suggested by asset-specific analysis.

In practice, designing rules that would eliminate precisely the transitional effects on wealth from fundamental tax reform is difficult for at least three reasons. First, asset values would both increase and decrease as a result of fundamental tax reform, depending on the cost-recovery schedule provided under present law and the age of the asset at the time of transition. Providing relief for losses in asset values, with no offsetting adjustment for windfall gains, would not only be expensive from the standpoint of tax revenues, but would not necessarily achieve any sensible equity objective.

Second, even if the policy objective were simply to eliminate windfall losses (with no recapture of windfall gains), the appropriate transition rule would generally depend on how the market adjusted to the postreform equilibrium. If the adjustment process were slow, declines in asset value would generally be smaller and would thus require less transitional relief.

Third, the provision of transitional relief at the business level could not address effects on wealth that were not borne by equity owners. A decline in the real value of assets because of an increase in the overall price level for consumer goods, as might occur under a national retail sales tax or VAT, would affect domestic bondholders as well as domestic shareholders (but not foreign shareholders). Transition relief provided at the entity level would not compensate bondholders and would overcompensate foreign shareholders.

Unless tax reform were made effective retroactive to the date when investors first anticipated enactment, the failure to provide transitional rules that eliminated losses in wealth would encourage taxpayers to delay or accelerate transactions to arbitrage between the current and anticipated tax systems. Thus, the cost of providing transition relief by statute might not be as great as expected, given the opportunity for taxpayers to avoid at least some wealth losses where tax reform was anticipated.

When tax reform is truly unanticipated, however, Auerbach and Kotlikoff (1987) have shown that the cost of providing transitional relief can significantly affect the gain in efficiency from reform through a consumption tax. Much of the efficiency gain appears to be from its apparent lump-sum tax on existing wealth. In the long run, however, the efficiency gain may be offset by the precedential effect of government policies resulting in significant losses of wealth—and creating long-term disincentives to holding wealth.

Some have suggested a gradual phase-in of a new tax system as a way to moderate transitional effects on wealth (see Treasury 1977). Such an approach would delay the full implementation of the reformed tax rules regarding new investments (along with the desired economic benefits). Such a phase-in would also increase the complexity of the transition as well as increase the opportunities for tax arbitrage.

Notes

1 . The proposal would also eliminate the taxation of investment income at the individual level. A summary of the proposal is provided at http://flattax.house.gov/.

2. Our discussion complements the analysis presented by Gentry and Hubbard (1996). They note that changes at the individual level eliminating

the taxation of dividends and capital gains may have a further beneficial effect on stock prices. Auerbach (1996) also notes several factors discussed here.

3.   Shaviro (2000) provides an extended analysis of the equity and efficiency of transition policy generally.

4 . This chapter focuses on changes that directly affect cash flow and asset values. Schwarz, Merrill, and Edwards (1998) investigate the effects of fundamental tax reform on financial statements.

5.   The market-to-book ratio is computed as the market value of equity divided by the value of shareholder's equity as recorded in financial statements.

6.   Auerbach and Kotlikoff (1983) clearly present this view.

7.   The one statistically significant finding for the dynamic effect is removed when controls for industry effects are included. In general, the statistical significance of the results may be overstated by failing to control for contemporaneous cross-correlation of returns within industries.

8.   The analysis of a switch to a retail sales tax is similar to our analysis for the flat tax. In the case of the retail sales tax, the tax is commonly thought to be passed on to consumers through higher (tax-inclusive) prices rather than through reduced factor incomes. If a proper account is made for changes in the real purchasing power of assets, the conclusions are similar.

9.   In actuality, at any point in time some expectation of tax reform—including changes in tax rates for income (both potential increases and decreases), change in capital cost-recovery allowances and tax credits, and a change in tax structure—exists. The effects of reform on asset prices would then depend on public expectations at the time of the reform.

10. Depreciation deductions are less accelerated under the alternative minimum tax for most equipment. For a description of the effects of the AMT on investment incentives, see Lyon 1997.

11. Most self-created intangible capital is expensed for tax purposes. Since 1993, the cost of newly acquired existing intangible assets, such as goodwill, customer lists, and trademarks, is generally amortized over fifteen years.

12. The present value of economic depreciation is $\delta/(\delta+r)$, where d is the rate of economic depreciation and r is the real after-tax rate of return.

13. A small amount of tangible capital is immediately written off for tax purposes. In 2000 the first $20,000 of equipment may be expensed for businesses undertaking less than $200,000 of investment. Under the Small Business Job Protection Act of 1996, the amount of investment eligible for expensing will increase to $25,000 in 2003.

14. The changes in asset value calculated for representative three-year, five-year, and seven-year assets are a function of the asset's rate of economic depreciation, which can vary within any asset class, in addition to the asset's recovery period. For illustrative purposes, the annual rate of economic depreciation is assumed to be 0.3125, 0.1316, and 0.0833 for assets in the three-

year, five-year, and seven-year classes, respectively. Table 3–2 provides additional detail.

15. More realistically, adjustment costs may partially restrict the amount of new investment undertaken and may limit the decline in the pretax value of capital services. The empirical results of Lyon (1989a), discussed in the section "Empirical Evidence from Prior Tax Reforms," suggest the possibility of periods when excess returns are earned on inframarginal new investment, although adjustment costs result in no excess return to marginal new investment.

16. With bankruptcy comes a probability that the bondholders would become the ultimate claimants of the firm's assets. If these assets have declined in value, then bondholders too bear some of the effect on asset prices. By changing after-tax cash flows, the consumption tax could also change the probability of default and could thereby alter the division of firm value between stockholders and bondholders.

17. Special rules would likely apply to financial intermediaries. See Merrill and Edwards 1996.

18. In contrast, Bradford (1996) suggests that owners of assets with short remaining lives would be most advantaged by permitting depreciation in a transition. Our results on the benefits of the transition in tables 3–7 through 3–9 differ from Bradford's, given the actual pattern of accelerated depreciation under the present law.

References

Auerbach, Alan J. 1989. "Tax Reform and Adjustment Costs: The Impact on Investment and Market Value." International Economic Review 30 (4) (November): 939–62.

———. 1996. "Tax Reform, Capital Allocation, Efficiency, and Growth." In Economic Effects of Fundamental Tax Reform, edited by Henry J. Aaron and William G. Gale. Washington, D.C.: Brookings Institution.

Auerbach, Alan J., and Dale W. Jorgenson. 1980. "Inflation-Proof Depreciation of Assets." Harvard Business Review 58 (5) (September–October): 113–18.

Auerbach, Alan J., and Laurence J. Kotlikoff. 1983. "Investment versus Savings Incentives: The Size of the Bang for the Buck and the Potential for Self-Financing Business Tax Cuts." In The Economic Consequences of Government Deficits, edited by Laurence H. Meyer. Boston: Kluwer-Nijoff.

———. 1987. Dynamic Fiscal Policy. Cambridge: Cambridge University Press.

Bradford, David F. 1996. "Consumption Taxes: Some Fundamental Transition Issues." In Frontiers of Tax Reform, edited by Michael J. Boskin. Stanford: Hoover Institution.

Bull, Nicholas, and Lawrence B. Lindsey. 1995. "Monetary Implications of Tax Reforms." *National Tax Journal* 49 (3): 359–80.

Cutler, David M. 1988. "Tax Reform and the Stock Market: An Asset Price Approach." *American Economic Review* 78 (5)(December): 1107–17.

Downs, Thomas, and Cuneyt Demirgures. 1992. "The Asset Price Theory of Shareholder Revaluations: Tests with the Tax Reforms of the 1980s." *Financial Review* 27 (2)(May): 151–84.

Downs, Thomas, and Hassan Tehranian 1988. "Predicting Stock Price Responses to Tax Policy Changes." *American Economic Review* 78 (5)(December): 1118–30.

Feldstein, Martin.1981. "The Tax Cut: Why the Market Dropped." *Wall Street Journal,* November 11.

Feldstein, Martin, and Charles Horioka.1980. "Domestic Saving and International Capital Flows." *Economic Journal* 90 (358)(June): 314–29.

Gentry, William, and R. Glenn Hubbard. 1996. "Distributional Implications of Introducing a Broad-Based Consumption Tax." National Bureau of Economic Research Working Paper 5832. Cambridge: NBER.

Graetz, Michael J. 1985. "Retroactivity Revisited." *Harvard Law Review* 98 (8) (June):1820.

Gravelle, Jane. 1984. "Effects of Changes in the Taxation of Income from Capital on Stockholders' Wealth and q." Mimeographed.

—————. 1995. "The Flat Tax and Other Tax Proposals: Who Will Bear the Tax Burden?" CRS Report for Congress 95-1141E, November 29. Washington, D.C.: Congressional Research Service.

Grubert, Harry, and Scott Newlon. 1995. "The International Implications of Consumption Tax Proposals." *National Tax Journal* 48 (4) (December): 619–47.

Hall, Robert E. 1996. "The Effects of Tax Reform on Prices and Asset Values." In *Tax Policy and the Economy,* edited by James M. Poterba. Cambridge: MIT Press.

Hall, Robert, and Alvin Rabushka. 1995. *The Flat Tax,* 2d ed. Palo Alto: Hoover Press.

Lyon, Andrew B. 1989a. "The Effect of the Investment Tax Credit on the Value of the Firm." *Journal of Public Economics* 38 (2): 227–47.

—————. 1989b. "Did ACRS Really Cause Stock Prices to Fall?" National Bureau of Economic Research Working Paper 2990. Cambridge: NBER.

—————. 1997. *Cracking the Code: Making Sense of the Corporate Alternative Minimum Tax.* Washington, D.C.: Brookings Institution.

Merrill, Peter, and Chris Edwards. 1996. "Cash-flow Taxation of Financial Services." *National Tax Journal* 49 (3) (September): 487–500.

Modigliani, Franco, and Merton H. Miller. 1963. "Corporate Income Taxes and the Cost of Capital: A Correction." *American Economic Review* 53 (June): 433–42.

Schwarz, Melbert, Peter Merrill, and Chris Edwards. 1998. "Transitional Issues in Fundamental tax Reform: A Financial Accounting Perspective." In *Tax Policy and the Economy*, vol. 12, edited by James M. Poterba. Cambridge: MIT Press.

Shaviro, Daniel. 2000. *When Rules Change: An Economic and Political Analysis of Transition Relief and Retroactivity*. Chicago: University of Chicago Press.

Summers, Lawrence H. 1981. "Taxation and Corporate Investment: A q-Theory Approach." *Brookings Papers on Economic Activity* (1): 67–127.

————. 1983. "The Asset Price Approach to the Analysis of Capital Income Taxation." In *Proceedings of the Seventy-Sixth Annual Conference*. Columbus, Ohio: National Tax Association–Tax Institute of America.

U.S. Department of the Treasury. 1977. *Blueprints for Basic Tax Reform*. Washington, D.C.: Government Printing Office.

Commentary

James R. Hines Jr.

Americans readily accept the notion that fundamental tax reform could entail significant income redistribution, even if the exact mechanisms for such redistribution remain confusing and obscure. Andrew Lyon and Peter Merrill analyze an important and difficult aspect of reform-induced redistribution: changes in the values of existing capital assets. They offer readers an excellent service in patiently and clearly tracing how asset values respond to tax changes. While their conclusion—that asset values might rise in response to fundamental tax reforms—is controversial, their method is sufficiently careful and transparent to permit readers to reformulate the model and draw their own conclusions if they do not like those provided.

The first insight in the analysis is that fundamental tax reforms encouraging new investment would simultaneously reduce the values of existing assets through natural competitive forces. For many analysts, this first step is also the last step. Lyon and Merrill instead march on and draw attention to three important aspects of fundamental tax reforms that maintain or enhance the values of existing assets. First, the authors note that reduced future statutory rates on corporate taxes would raise the values of existing assets by permitting asset owners to retain higher fractions of their profits. Second, they argue that any complementarities between old and new assets would raise existing asset values when tax reforms encouraged new investment. Third, they point out that rising adjustment costs would in any case dampen the effect of fundamental tax reforms on the volume of new investment and would thereby preserve, or in some cases augment, the market values of existing assets.

Discussions of the merits of fundamental tax reform typically overlook those three considerations, despite their potential importance. As Lyon and Merrill argue, the three points generally imply that any reductions in asset prices that accompanied such reforms would be smaller than typically assumed.

However, a fundamental disconnect arises between the considerations raised by Lyon and Merrill and the effects of fundamental tax reforms that would make them appealing to advocates. Indeed, the major point of fundamental tax reform is to improve the incentives for saving and investment. The considerations that Lyon and Merrill identify as preserving the values of existing assets would also dampen the effects of fundamental tax reform on the size of the capital stock.

It is useful to consider each of these effects separately. Lyon and Merrill argue first that because a large fraction of asset values would reflect returns to intangible assets, reform-induced reductions in statutory rates for corporate taxes would greatly increase aggregate asset values. That conclusion is plausible because profitable firms would certainly benefit from reductions in statutory tax rates. It is essential to this argument, however, that profitability persist in the wake of tax reform, and thus the essential qualifier "intangible" on the assets. Owners of tangible assets would benefit from reductions in statutory tax rates but for the fact that the tax change would encourage new investment that would subsequently generate output that would compete with output produced by the old capital. To the extent that intangible capital consisted of items that were difficult to replicate, such as successful patents, trademarks, reputations, and good fortune in hiring and retaining the right employees, then its product might not lose value from competitive goods and services produced with new capital.

Of course, fundamental tax reform might not encourage the development of such intangible capital. The ability to take immediate expensing for plant and equipment investment would not stimulate the development of intangible capital if such capital were the product of labor-intensive development. Fundamental tax reform would not be likely to lead to the creation of many new software companies in which investment expenses consisted almost exclusively of wages and salaries: tax reform would not change the effective tax rates on such investment. Consequently, to the extent that intangible capital was as important a component of the total capital stock as Lyon and Merrill argue, fundamental tax reform would not lead to a major expansion in capital formation.

Second, Lyon and Merrill observe that owners of existing capital would benefit from the reduced future effective tax rates on new investment because those owners would make some of the new investment. The argument is correct if the favorable tax treatment of new investment is a source of profitability. Would it be? Under standard conditions, favorable tax treatment would not generate profits for investors because competitive forces would drive pre-tax returns to the point where investments would earn only normal after-tax rates of return. Fundamental tax reform would generate rents to holders of existing capital only if benefiting from new investment required owning existing capital—in other words, only if old capital and new capital were complements. Certainly, a complementary relationship might exist between old and new capital. But the existence of such complementarity would greatly dampen the effect of tax reform on new investment because complementarity is a symmetric relationship. Complementarity between old capital and new capital would imply that the limited stock of old capital generated diminishing returns to new investment and thereby reduced the extent to which aggregate investment rose in response to fundamental tax reform.

Lyon and Merrill's third consideration is that the costs of a rapid adjustment of capital stocks would raise the value of old capital during periods of rapid capital accumulation; such a condition would characterize the years following fundamental tax reform. The argument is correct, although once again its thrust is to reduce the implied reaction of capital investment to the incentives introduced by tax reforms.

Each of those three considerations would act to preserve the values of existing assets in the wake of fundamental tax reform and would also reduce the stimulatory effects of tax reform on new investment. Competitive forces in the economy seem to make this trade-off fundamental because new investment and the economic activity that accompanies it necessarily compete with the product of existing capital and thereby lower the rents attributable to it.

Two of the more specific arguments advanced by Lyon and Merrill deserve close examination. First, the intangible nature of business capital implies that fundamental tax reform would not encourage the development of substitutes. But fundamental tax reform would stimulate new spending on depreciable assets such as plants and equipment. Because business operations often produce the intangible capital, much of the investment in which firms depreciate, as well as the kind of investment incentives generated by fundamental tax reform, indirectly encourages the development of new intangible capital. The new intangible capital would compete in the marketplace with existing intangible capital and would thereby reduce the value of existing assets.

The automobile industry offers an instructive example. American automobile companies certainly possess intangible capital in such forms as business experience, relationships with dealers and suppliers, brand names, and customer loyalty. Share prices reflect the value of that intangible capital. Fundamental tax reform would reduce the cost of new plant and equipment investment and might thereby encourage foreign automobile manufacturers to establish new plants in the United States. The added competition would reduce the margins that American companies can earn on sales and would thereby reduce the value of their intangible capital.

The second argument concerns the ability of adjustment costs to preserve asset values in the wake of fundamental tax reform. Although adjustment costs could certainly have this effect, assessing the likelihood of that effect is difficult because existing estimates of adjustment costs reflect the difficulty of estimating the determinants of investment as much as they do the costs of putting new capital in place. In a standard specification of an investment equation, a sluggish response of new investment to changed incentives would be interpreted as reflecting the existence of important adjustment costs. Consequently, any misspecification of an investment equation—the omission of important variables, the mismeasurement of important variables, the failure to include an appropriate number of lags, and so on—would likely generate major implied adjustment costs. Existing investment equations are certainly misspecified along several of these dimensions. Although estimated adjustment costs at hand are useful when forecasting the effects of tax reforms, the magnitudes of actual adjustment costs are basically unknown, as is, therefore, their ability to preserve existing asset values after fundamental tax reform.

Lyon and Merrill fight a good fight. Their insight is that the reactions of asset prices to fundamental tax reform would not correspond exactly to the valuation changes predicted by simple models. More specifically, the authors predict higher equity values in the short run following tax reform, and they identify several important considerations that all point in this direction. All the considerations advanced by Lyon and Merrill would dampen the effect of fundamental tax reform on the capital stock. Because an important motivation behind enacting fundamental tax reform is to increase the size of the economy's capital stock, Lyon and Merrill draw attention to an important and fundamental trade-off between preserving asset values and pursuing the goals of the fundamental reform of the nation's tax system.

4

Will a Consumption Tax Kill the Housing Market?

Donald Bruce
and
Douglas Holtz-Eakin

Widespread negative perceptions about the federal income tax system—that it has become a burdensome source of economic inefficiency, is unfair, and is administratively unworkable—have spawned numerous calls to replace the income tax with a comprehensive consumption-based tax. Taxation on the basis of consumption would shift the locus of the tax system from the generation of economic resources to the consumption of economic benefits, would level the playing field between consumption at different stages of the life cycle, and would equalize the tax treatment of alternative assets (see, for example, Hall and Rabushka 1995). As a matter of course, however, equalizing the tax treatment of all investment

We thank Stacy Dickert-Conlin, James Follain, Kevin Hassett, Patric Hendershott, R. Glenn Hubbard, Allison Ivory, William Gale, Mary Lovely, James Poterba, Mark Skidmore, and John Yinger for useful comments on earlier versions of this research. The manuscript has benefited from the efforts of seminar participants at the American Enterprise Institute, the National Tax Association, the Southern Economic Association, and Syracuse University. We are indebted to the Center for Policy Research, Syracuse University, for research support and to Esther Gray for her aid in preparing the manuscript.

vehicles would eliminate the tax-favored status of owner-occupied housing—a reform at odds with both the history of taxation in the United States and conventional political wisdom. The deductibility of mortgage interest and state and local property taxes can be traced to the inaugural federal income tax in 1913.

The durability of the preferential tax treatment of owner-occupied housing reflects the widespread fear that reform (seemingly *any* reform) would harm the property values of homeowners. Consumption-based reforms are portrayed as especially threatening and raise the specter of a massive decline in housing values, substantial windfall losses in the housing wealth of U.S. households, and large-scale defaults on mortgage obligations. In an early and widely publicized study, Data Resources Incorporated (DRI) predicted an apocalyptic fall in housing values; it estimated that a flat tax would result in an aggregate decline of 15 percent, equivalent to a loss of $1.7 trillion in housing equity (see Brinner, Lansky, and Wyss 1995).

Should the public believe this? Such a forecast would be convincing if it stemmed from a careful analysis of the behavior of the housing market. But the DRI analysis does not reflect any, much less sophisticated, economic behavior. Instead, the forecast $1.7 trillion decline in housing values is simply the present value of the benefits lost by the elimination of the deductions for mortgage interest and property taxes.[1]

A step in the right direction is the conventional, static analysis of Capozza, Green, and Hendershott (1996), which reaches conclusions similar to those of DRI. The authors assume that tax reform would not change the user cost—the conceptually correct rental-equivalent price—of owner-occupied housing; they calculate the change in housing values on this basis. However, if the prices were unchanged, then the quantity of housing purchased would also remain fixed. Thus, the assumptions in a conventional user-cost analysis imply that fundamental tax reform would have absolutely no impact on the size of the housing sector. Put differently: the tax-favored treatment of residential housing has not induced any economic distortion; this conclusion is at odds with both casual introspection and a large body of research.

We revisit the impact on housing values by a reform through a consumption tax: we use a framework that reflects economic decisionmaking by households (buying more when prices decline; buying less when they rise) and rational valuation of houses as assets. Moreover, because the key aspect of reforms is a mandatory transition from one tax regime to another, we focus on the dynamics of the transition in the housing market, in addition to the longer-term repercussions of tax reform.

A reform through a consumption tax could raise the market value of existing homes, even though the reform eliminated tax-based subsidies. Consider a simple example in which individuals do not itemize deductions of mortgage interest or property taxes (40 percent of homeowners do not) and in which the consumption tax takes the form of a 20 percent value-added tax (VAT). Eliminating deductions would obviously have no direct impact on existing homeowners in these circumstances, while the VAT would raise the cost of new homes by 20 percent. Older, existing homes would enjoy a tax-based advantage of 20 percent, leading to a rise in their value, *ceteris paribus*.[2]

Over the longer term, the natural process of new construction, rental conversions, the razing of existing dwellings, and other market adjustments would eliminate the distinction between existing and new homes, and the price differential along with it. But during transition, the tax reform would have the perhaps surprising effect of enhancing the value of older homes. To the extent that households itemized, the loss of deductibility would mitigate that effect, but the underlying tendency would remain.

Our goal is to put some meat on this skeletal insight with a formal, numerical simulation model emphasizing the economic fundamentals of the aggregate housing market. Before doing so, we revisit the facts of size and composition of the U.S. housing market. Next we summarize the key features of some of the leading proposals for tax reform, with an emphasis on their common features. Then we sketch the economic framework for our tax analysis, the key results detailed next. After revisiting our analysis with an eye toward distributional issues and the realities of implementing tax reform, we summarize the analysis.

The U.S. Residential Housing Sector

Residential housing is an important element of the U.S. economy. First, there is a lot of it. The *Statistical Abstract of the United States* reports that in 1995 the value of fixed reproducible wealth in residential housing was $7.7 trillion, constituting nearly 50 percent of private capital ($15.7 trillion) and 34 percent of total fixed wealth ($22.6 trillion). And much of this wealth lies in the hands of homeowners. Again, with 1995 to give a sense of comparable magnitudes, the owner-occupancy rate (as a fraction of all occupied households) was 64.7 percent, a figure that has been stable over the 1990s.

However, the new activity in the housing market—despite its absolute size—is a less important part of the annual economy. Between 1995 and 1997, residential investment constituted only a bit more than one-quarter (28 percent) of annual private gross fixed investment. Accordingly, the housing sector draws only a minor part of the economic resources available for investment, and increases or decreases in this demand would likely be accommodated without great pressure on the costs of capital. As another reflection of this fact, 667,000 new privately owned one-family housing units were sold in 1995, compared with sales of 3,812,000 existing one-family housing units. In other words, sales of new homes accounted for slightly less than 15 percent of all sales in 1995.

The moral for housing market analysis is twofold. First, sales of both new homes—one-quarter of fixed investment, or 15 percent of home sales, is nothing to sneeze at—and of existing homes must be analyzed simultaneously. Second, analyzing the housing market can be done without the complication of tracing the performance of the economy as a whole.

Tax Treatment of Housing and Consumption-Based Reform

The current system gives owner-occupied housing a tax preference. The fundamental source of this tax preference is the exclusion of imputed rent (or the service value of the home) from the income tax base. If one owns a home and rents it to others, the rent is included in the income tax base. However, if that homeowner in effect rents the property to himself by occupying it, the implicit, or imputed, rent payments are not counted toward taxable income. In the language of consumption-based reform, the consumption of housing services (for which one would pay imputed rent to oneself) would not be taxed. Clearly, the objective of consumption-based tax reform is to include housing (and all other) consumption in the tax base. In that way, consumption-based reform would eliminate the tax preference toward owner-occupied housing.

The income tax system has three other effects on housing decisions. First, property tax payments are deductible. To the extent that those taxes are properly viewed as payments for consumption benefits provided by local governments, deductibility lowers the price of the consumption relative to direct payments or nontax payment for these services. Reform through a consumption tax would eliminate deductibility and would level the playing field with respect to government-provided consumption.

Second, mortgage interest payments are deductible and lead to a subsidy to debt-financing, *ceteris paribus*. Of course, to take advantage of the subsidy, homeowners must itemize deductions on their income tax returns. As a result, the effective size of the subsidy is the amount by which mortgage interest exceeds the standard deduction (in contrast to total mortgage interest deductions). Similarly, if individuals itemize their deductions, the provision lowers the cost of additional debt-financed housing and distorts marginal incentives. The same is not true, however, if homeowners employ the standard deduction. We return to this issue below.

Third, capital gains on housing are essentially untaxed and constitute a reduced tax on housing equity returns, *ceteris paribus*. Because consumption-based systems would not tax the return to saving and investment, such reforms would equalize the treatments of all assets. With respect to housing in particular, mortgage interest deductibility would be eliminated while the nontaxation of capital gains would be retained.

In sum, the transition to a consumption-based system may be disentangled into two separate steps. First, the elimination of deductibility would level the playing field with respect to asset returns and government-provided consumption. Second, the taxation of imputed rent, or housing consumption services, would bring housing into the consumption tax base.

In practice, reforms would implement those steps in a variety of ways. The most direct would be a national retail sales tax, which would entail a tax on the purchase of a new home—and would thereby raise its price.[3] Similarly, the consumption tax could be implemented as a value-added tax (VAT); again, the reform would appear in the housing market as a tax on transactions in the construction and sale of new homes.[4] Finally, proposals for a flat tax, derived from the work of Robert Hall and Alvin Rabushka, may best be viewed as a VAT in which taxes on the wage base would be collected at the household level, while taxes on the remainder of value added would continue to be collected at the firm level.[5] The latter component would effectively raise the price of new housing; the increase would be the equivalent of paying in advance a stream of future taxes on the annual consumption value of the shelter services provided by the house. Because of the popularity of the flat tax and its variants, we focus on this as our model consumption tax reform. At the same time, our results are more general than such a focus might seem to imply: the purest form of the flat tax would have the *same* economic effects as either a VAT or a national retail sales tax at the same rate.

A Framework for Tax Analysis

At the heart of tax reform proposals is the notion that the fully phased-in reformed tax system would be economically superior to the existing income tax. Accordingly, any framework for tax analysis should be capable of capturing the long-run effects of fundamental tax reform. But at the same time, the political economy of reform demands an assessment of the transitional and phase-in effects of the reform. With respect to housing, the conventional analysis is an odd and inappropriate mix of these two approaches. First, the total amount of housing is typically viewed as *fixed;* this condition suggests that the analysis is suitable only for a very short period (or is based on the transparently counterfactual notion that the U.S. housing market is not subject to swings in building activity). At the same time, the effects on prices are portrayed as permanent ones, with the implication that these price swings are consistent with the long-term outlook. In fact, neither is likely to prevail during a reform.

Instead, we employ an approach that yields not only the permanent, long-term impacts on the residential housing market but also the dynamic adjustment path for the value of housing during the postreform transition.[6] We begin with the observation that housing has a dual role: (1) it is a consumption good in the same way as food, clothing, and other necessities and (2) it is an investment vehicle. Because of the second role, competition in the asset market demands that homeowners be compensated for holding their house in a way comparable to the after-tax return on alternative investments. However, because of the first role, part of the return takes the form of consumption benefits—the valuation of the services the house provides as a shelter. In short, if $i(1 - \tau)$ is the after-tax return on an alternative investment (for example, a taxable, interest-bearing bond), then the return offered by housing must meet the hurdle

$$i(1 - \tau) = \frac{\frac{S}{H} - [t_p (1 - \tau) + \delta + m] P_H}{P_H} + \frac{\Delta P_H}{P_H} \qquad (4\text{--}1)$$

where i is the nominal rate of return, τ is the individual's marginal income tax rate, S is the implicit service flow (also known as the imputed rent) from ownership, H is the amount of housing, t_p is the property tax rate, δ is the percentage rate of depreciation, m is the percentage rate of maintenance costs, ΔP_H is the price of a house, and ΔP_H is the change in the value of the house, that is, the capital gain on housing. Thus, the return to housing comes in two forms. The first is nonfinancial and is measured by the consumption benefits net of property tax, depreciation, and maintenance costs. The second, financial, return is the (untaxed) capital gain on housing.[7] Because that return reflects both investors' preferences for assets and homeowners' demands for shelter, equation 4–1 effectively captures the demand for owner-occupied housing. Because houses might be subject to capital gains or losses during market transitions, the equation captures equally well the long-term demand (when prices stabilize and capital gains are eliminated) and the short-term demand (in the face of fluctuations in house prices).

Of course, we require a supply curve as well to track the evolution of the market. We capture the incentives to builders by noting that new construction (C) (or increases in the housing stock) becomes greater when building houses is more profitable; that is, when house prices (or values) rise compared with the construction or replacement cost:

$$C \equiv \Delta H = \Phi (P_H) H. \qquad (4\text{--}2)$$

Taken together, equations 4–1 and 4–2 comprise a standard, dynamic, asset-market–oriented model of tax analysis.

Aggregate Impacts of Tax Reform

As noted, consumption-based tax reforms could be enacted in a variety of equivalent forms: as a national retail sales tax, as a VAT, or as one of several descendants of the flat tax. Because of the convenience of the equivalence, we focus on the flat tax here. The discussion above also indicated the usefulness of thinking of two steps in a consumption-based reform: (1) the elimination of deductibility, followed by (2) the taxation of housing consumption benefits. We also discuss the effects of a partial reform that stops at the first step: the elimination of deductions for mortgage interest and property taxes.

To implement our approach (details are in the appendix), we must adopt a solution technique, particular functional forms for housing demand and sup-ply, and numerical values for key parameters. For the present purposes, the key feature of our approach is the focus on a representative homeowner. That is, our model is well suited for describing the typical effects in the overall mar-ket. It is not explicitly designed to analyze particular submarkets (for exam-ple, vacation homes), although we touch briefly on issues of distribution below.

Our representative homeowner faces a property tax at a rate of 1.4 percent and is presented with maintenance and depreciation that average 3.0 percent of the value of the house. He has a marginal tax rate of 0.22, which would fall to 0.194 when deductibility is removed and to 0.17 under the flat tax.[8] We set the loan-to-value ratio at 0.4 and assume that 60 percent of mortgage interest and property taxes are deducted. Those assumptions accurately cap-ture the marginal incentives when 40 percent of homeowners do not itemize. However, the assumptions do not recognize the impact of the availability of the standard deduction in reducing the total subsidy provided by the deductibility of mortgage interest.

Our nominal interest rate is 7.5 percent, roughly in line with current con-ditions. For the week ending October 2, 1998, the primary mortgage survey of the Federal Home Loan Mortgage Corporation (Freddie Mac) indicated that the thirty-year fixed-rate mortgage (FRM) averaged 6.60 percent, with fees and points averaging 1.0. One year earlier, the thirty-year FRM average was 7.31 percent.

Turning to the key behavioral parameters, we choose the (inverse price) elasticity of demand for housing services to be $\eta = -2.0$, but we vary this value between -0.5 and -3.0 to gauge the impact of this parameter on the results. On the supply side, we use a baseline elasticity of construction with respect to P_H of 0.8. Again, however, because the responsiveness of new construction to the alterations in the tax regime is central to the dynamics of the housing market, we vary this elasticity between 0.1 and 0.9.[9]

We present the results of simulating the reforms in a series of figures. The simulations provide two types of responses: long-run changes in the housing market and the transitional dynamics of adjusting from the existing tax system to the reform setting. Although it is not the primary focus of this study, we begin with the former before turning to an analysis of the adjustment paths.

TABLE 4–1
Changes from Initial to New Steady States

	Remove Deductibility		Flat Tax	
	Percent change in P_H	Percent change in H	Percent change in P_H	Percent change in H
Baseline (ε=0.8, η=-2; β=0.4)	0	-1.9	17.0	- 8.0
η=-0.5	0	-3.8	17.0	-15.5
η=1.0	0	-2.8	17.0	-11.8
η=2.5	0	-1.6	17.0	- 6.9
η=-3.0	0	-1.4	17.0	- 6.1

NOTE: ε = structure supply elasticity; η = inverse elasticity of housing demand; β = loan-to-value ratio. Percentage changes for various values of ε are identical to those in the baseline case.

Our examination of long-run responses begins in table 4–1.[10] As shown, the tax regime directly dictates the steady-state changes in the value of P_H. Under the flat tax, the steady-state value of P_H would rise by a percentage equal to the business-level tax on new construction.[11]   Simply removing deductibility would have no effect on P_H.

In contrast, the contraction in the quantity of housing differs markedly across the two reforms. Consider the first row of the table, which shows the results of removing the deductions for mortgage interest and property taxes. The reform would induce an eventual decline of 1.9 percent in the housing stock. In contrast, the flat tax results in a greater long-term decline of 8 percent. In short, removing the tax subsidy for owner-occupied housing and taxing it directly would lead to a smaller housing stock. Although that qualitative result is not unsurprising, it is at odds with previous analyses of reforms. Also, because the flat tax would raise the effective price of housing consumption more dramatically, it would have a greater effect on the quantity demanded.[12]

As noted, despite the magnitude of the housing market in absolute terms, it constitutes a relatively small fraction of the new flow of capital investment. Thus, the long-run supply of housing could, one assumes, be expanded without price increases. For that reason, the replacement cost would be constant, and changes in the parameters of the construction function would not affect the simulations. Alternative assumptions regarding the behavior of housing demand, however, would influence the nature of the steady state. To give the reader a feel for the issue, the rows of the table show the effect of varying the price sensitivity of demand embodied in the value of η. A look across the columns indicates that varying the behavior does not alter the

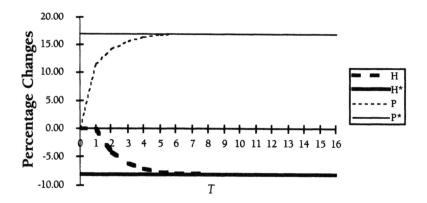

FIGURE 4–1

Impact of Removing Deductions for Mortgage Interest and
Property Taxes

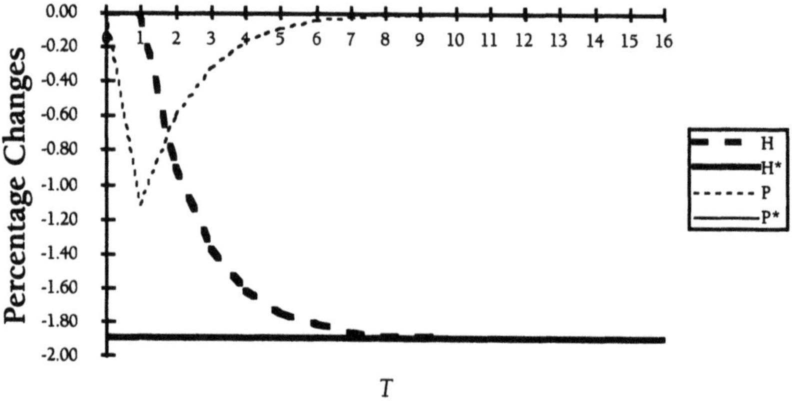

Figure 4–2

Impact of Flat Tax

ordering of the effects of the reforms on the housing stock. Glancing down rows, however, points to the effect on the magnitude of the impact of tax reform. As the demand for housing becomes more price sensitive with respect to the user cost (that is, as η grows in absolute value), the decline in the stock of housing lessens. Not surprisingly, the more elastic the demand, the greater the impact of introducing a tax is.

These results are useful for gauging the long-term pressures introduced by tax reform. At the heart of the issue, however, are the short-run dynamics of the housing market as engendered by a reform. Figure 4–1 shows the simulated impact of removing deductions for mortgage interest and property taxes. The immediate effect would be a reduction in housing values, a result consistent with both conventional wisdom and our economic framework. However, the magnitude of the decline would be only a bit more than one percentage point and would be reversed relatively quickly.[13] In contrast, the figure indicates that the size of the residential housing sector would fall steadily and reach a long-term reduction of about 2 percent. Of course, that is precisely the idea behind the efficiency gains from tax reform: existing subsidies have produced a housing sector that is "too large." Efficiency-enhancing reforms would channel economic resources elsewhere in the economy.

As noted, removing deductions would be only one part of a fundamental reform such as a flat tax. As shown in figure 4–2, however, our simulation of the effects does not suggest a dramatic decline in housing values. Instead, the short-run impact would be for prices to *rise* by roughly 10 percent and ultimately by 17 percent.[14] Our earlier discussion suggests precisely that response. The decline because of the loss of deductions would be more than offset by the positive impact on prices of the business-level tax.

Figures 4–1 and 4–2 focus on the level of housing prices and on comparisons between old and new housing. Because fundamental tax reform, however, might affect the prices of other goods as well—and thus the overall price level—ascertaining the real value of housing wealth might become more difficult. For example, Besley and Rosen (1998) find that sales taxes are often incorporated into sales prices at a rate exceeding 100 percent. In this context, new housing prices might rise by far more than 17 percent and thereby draw up the prices of existing homes by a greater amount than shown in figure 4–2. At the same time, the impact on the consumer price of other goods might be less than 100 percent. (One could imagine as well reverse scenarios in which the price of a nonhousing good would rise by more than 17 percent, but the price of housing by less.) In short, while that issue is important, its net effect on the analysis is far from obvious and is not resolved here.

Figures 4–1 and 4–2 embody the bad news–goods news of fundamental reform. The bad news is that the elimination of the tax subsidies for housing would place downward pressure on house prices. The good news is that the introduction of a consumption tax on new housing would enhance the value of existing homes. That result might make the distributional effects of tax reform more palatable, while the increased cost of new homes would channel scarce capital to other, more valuable uses in the economy.

Robustness of Results. Our numerical simulations reinforce the qualitative story in the introduction. The numbers themselves, however, are the outcome of our particular decisions regarding parameter values and the economic environment. An exhaustive summary of the numerical implications of changing

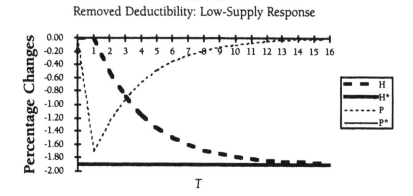

FIGURE 4–3
Removed Deductibility: Low-Supply Response

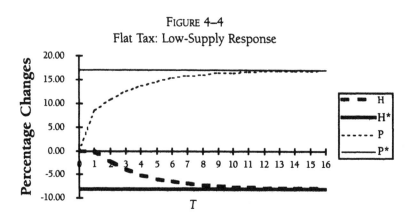

FIGURE 4–4
Flat Tax: Low-Supply Response

each parameter is beyond the scope of (our patience and) this chapter. However, in figures 4–3 and 4–4 we focus on the implications of assuming a highly unresponsive housing supply.

We do so for two reasons. First, the conventional analysis assumes a completely unresponsive supply. That situation strikes us as unrealistic, but gauging the effects of a fairly unresponsive supply might be useful. Second, the supply response to the nature of fundamental reform would be a *contraction* in the housing sector. Because scant empirical experience with that phenomenon exists, our understanding of its magnitude is accordingly thin. Introspection suggests to some that the response would be quite slow and difficult—we must wait for houses to fall down. However, to others the adjustment would be relatively painless and quick—houses could leave the homeowner sector through the stroke of a lawyer's pen and could become commercial buildings or rental units.

In any event, to gain a feel for the impact, we used a much lower value of the supply elasticity, ε— 0.3 instead of 0.8—to recompute our simulated reforms. Comparing figure 4–3 with figure 4–1 indicates that the lowered responsiveness would generate a greater initial decline and a slower convergence with the new long-run equilibrium. However, the main message appears to be that, with plausible parameter values, implications of removing deductions are quite modest for the housing market. A similar lesson emerges from comparing figures 4–2 and 4–4. Again, a less responsive construction industry would lead to stronger downward pressure on prices—in this case a smaller rise—and slower adjustment to the ultimate size of the housing sector.

As another possibility, we may have simply stacked the deck on the demand side by giving our representative homeowners too low a tax rate (and thus low valuation of deductions) or too few deductions (and thus indifference to deductions at all). To guard against that possibility, we show, in figures 4–5 and 4–6, the dynamic adjustments to tax reform under worst-case conditions. To maximize the impact of the loss of deductible mortgage interest, we assume that all homeowners itemize their deductions and that each home is fully mortgaged (the loan-to-value ratio, β, is 1.0). Both assumptions are clearly unrealistic but identify the upper bound of the size of deductions. Moreover, we make the deductions as valuable as possible by focusing on the homes of the well-to-do: we assume that all households have a marginal tax rate of 39.6 percent. For the *coup de grâce*, we assume that the supply response is unrealistically minimal (ε is set equal to 0.1) and that the household demand is extremely price sensitive (η is equal to -0.5).

The numerical implications of our choices are that housing prices are forecast to fall by roughly 18 percent in response to the loss of deductions (see figure 4–5) and to recover much more slowly. Similarly (see figure 4–6), in such circumstances the move to a consumption tax would result in a decline of 12 percent in housing prices, in contrast to the earlier upward pressures. In one interpretation of these results, the disaster in the housing market indicated by the conventional analysis could prevail only under the most unlikely combination of circumstances. More charitably, while the aggregate housing market would be relatively unaffected, one might expect particular market segments to respond more to tax reform.

Important Secondary Effects. Consistent with our focus on the housing market in isolation from the larger economy, the discussion thus far has assumed that reform through a consumption tax would not change either economywide conditions (we use a constant interest rate) or financial practices (we keep the loan-to-value ratio constant). Those suppositions are valuable in isolating the impacts of reform in our partial equilibrium model. But they are at odds with the larger setting of a fundamental tax reform. Specifically, it has been argued that interest rates would fall in the presence of a flat tax and that homeowners would reduce their mortgage debt in the absence of deductions. Consequently, examining the extent to which those economywide repercussions of tax reform would affect our

FIGURE 4–5
Worst-Case Scenario after Removal of Deduction

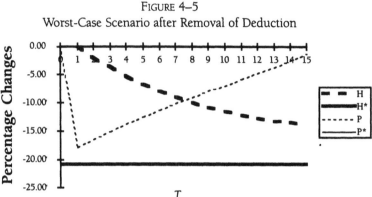

FIGURE 4–6
Worst-Case Scenario under Flat Tax

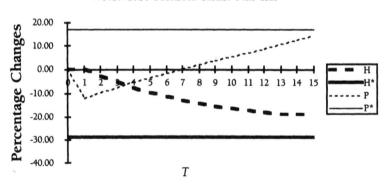

simulations of the transition would be interesting.

To this end, in figure 4–7 we present a variant of our baseline simulation of the flat tax in which the interest rate falls (as suggested by Hall and Rabushka 1995) and the loan-to-value ratio is reduced (see Follain and Melamed 1998). We allow the interest rate to fall by one percentage point (to 6.5 percent) and the loan-to-value ratio to fall by ten percentage points (to 30 percent). As anticipated, those secondary changes in the economy would mitigate the narrow repercussions in the housing market diagramed in figure 4–2. House prices would adjust more quickly to the long-term levels, and the long-term decline in the size of the housing stock—previously 8 percent—would be only about 5 percent. In summary, to the extent that interest rates fell and homeowners reduced their mortgage debt in response to tax reform, the effects on the housing market would be reduced.

FIGURE 4–7
Interest Rate and Loan-to-Value Reductions under Flat Tax

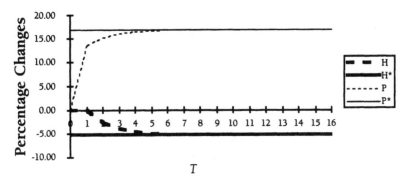

Distributional Effects

Our analysis has focused on the aggregate effects of tax reform on the housing market and suggests that the detrimental *overall* impact of consumption-based reform might be less frightening than previously advertised. However, introspection suggests that actual experiences would lie in a range that would be either more beneficial or somewhat more extreme than the overall average. And as the discussion of the worst-case scenario highlighted, the latter possibility could be a sobering reality to those households that had high income and property tax rates, itemized their deductions, and were highly leveraged. In short, the impact on affluent households would likely be greater (in percentage terms) than that on lower-income households.

As an impediment to tax reform, however, that insight stands conventional distributional politics on its head. Strangely, proponents of retaining the income tax—typically on the ground that a consumption tax would be regressive—base their support (at least in part) on the effects of reform on the housing market, when in fact those effects would increase the progressivity of a consumption tax. Moreover, the effects on the affluent would be the greatest precisely because existing tax subsidies most distort the housing decisions of the affluent. In sum, reform would enhance both efficiency and progressivity precisely because of the relatively major impacts on the affluent.

Tax Reform: Now and Forever?

To this point, a tax reform that happens now and lasts forever has framed our analysis. In technical terms, the tax reform is considered as unanticipated and permanent. In reality, tax reforms are widely debated and anticipated, and none has lasted forever. How do these features affect our conclusions?

Consider first the ability to anticipate the enactment of a major reform. During the period of debate and drafting, participants in the housing market would begin to revalue existing houses in light of the potential tax code. Thus, to the extent that their values would rise, the increases in the market prices would predate the actual enactment of the tax reform. Similarly, to the extent that the reform slowed new construction, builders would cut back in anticipation of a building slowdown. In short, the ability to foresee a reform would permit the market to adjust in advance of the reform, with the likely outcome that any price changes would be spread over a longer period. That reaction would lessen the likelihood of any scenario characterized by sharp, cataclysmic price changes.

Similarly, to the extent that the tax reform was viewed as less than permanent, a mixture of two views would drive actual prices: the "correct" prices under the current system and the "correct" prices under the tax reform. Accordingly, any suspicion that the pendulum might swing back toward the income tax would reduce the extent of the changes in prices and the supply of building.

Summary

Our goal has been to combine a rigorous economic model of the aggregate owner-occupied housing market with a numerical simulation model crafted to elucidate the likely transitional and long-term impacts of fundamental tax reform. Although the extent ultimately lies in the eye of the beholder, we conclude that the price impacts of even a fundamental reform of the federal income tax would likely be relatively modest. For that reason, concerns over the impact of tax reform on housing values and household net worth are almost certainly overstated and, to the extent that reform is otherwise desirable, should not impede reform. And perhaps we should not be surprised. As Gale (1997) points out, the British tax system has steadily scaled back tax preferences for housing with no noticeable impact on the housing market.

Appendix
Simulation Methods, Functional Forms, and Parameter Values

Solution Method. We solve the model in three steps. First, focusing on percentage changes we work with a version of the model in which the variables of interest (for example, housing prices and quantities) are entered as logarithms. Next, we linearize (in logs) the model in the vicinity of the postreform steady-state values and compute our simulations with the linearized version. Finally, we compute our perfect-foresight transition paths. Specifically, using an iterative search, we calculate the initial decline or jump in asset prices such that the entire subsequent sequence of changes in asset prices leads precisely to the postreform steady state.

Functional Forms and Parameter Values. The basic parameters are shown in panel A of table 4–A1. We assume that the representative homeowner faces a property tax at a rate of 1.4 percent and that maintenance and depreciation average 3.0 percent of the house value. Also, we assume that the service flow and housing stock are linked by the constant elasticity function

$$S = S_0 H^\eta$$

where is a constant and $\varepsilon < 0$ is the inverse price elasticity of demand. Our settings for the parameters of the function are also shown in the table. For our baseline simulations, we choose the (inverse price) elasticity of demand for housing services to be $\varepsilon = -2.0$, but we vary this value between -0.5 and -3.0 to gauge the impact of this parameter on the simulations. On the supply side, we use a baseline elasticity of construction with respect to P_H (η) of 0.8. Again, however, because the responsiveness of new construction to the alterations in the tax regime would be central to the dynamics of the housing market, we vary this elasticity between 0.1 and 0.9.

We model two reforms: (1) a partial reform, eliminating the deductibility of mortgage interest and property taxes, and (2) the variant of the flat tax proposed by Congressman Armey and Senator Shelby. For purposes of comparison, we follow closely the choices of Capozza, Green, and Hendershott (1996) in choosing our numerical parameter values for these reforms, shown in panel B of table 4–A1.

We set the nominal pretax interest rate at 7.5 percent and assume that the tax reform does not affect it. Considerable debate concerns the impact of tax reform on interest rates; our goal is to focus on the act of reform itself and abstract from ancillary economic impacts. *Ceteris paribus,* that choice likely serves to maximize the negative impacts of tax reform because any reduction in interest rates would raise housing values. Following Capozza, Green, and Hendershott, we set the average marginal tax rate in the current system at 0.22. When simulating the effects of removing deductions in a revenue-neutral framework, we again follow their guidance and employ a rate of 0.194. We set the tax rate for the flat tax at 0.17.

As noted in Capozza, Green, and Hendershott, roughly 40 percent of homeowners do not itemize; we set the fraction of mortgage interest and property tax deductible equal to 0.60. Because none of the reforms would allow a deduction for mortgage interest, we set $\Theta = 0$. Similarly, property taxes lose their deductible status under both reforms examined.

The next two rows of the table show the financing and construction cost of housing, respectively. To focus on the real valuation of assets, we fix the loan-to-value ratio (β, above) at 0.4 throughout. We assume that the (normalized) replacement cost of a unit of housing is exogenously set at 1.0. Under the flat tax, the business-level tax raises the tax-inclusive break-even replacement cost

TABLE 4A–1
Parameter Values

Panel A

Parameter	Value
Property tax rate t_p	0.014
Housing supply elasticity (ε)	0.8
Inverse price elasticity of demand (η)	-2.0
Maintenance and depreciation ($m + \delta$)	0.03

Panel B

Parameter	Original	Deductibility Removed	Flat Tax
Interest rate (i)	0.075	0.075	0.075
Average marginal income tax rate (τ)	0.220	0.194	0.170
Percent of mortgage interest deductible (Θ)	0.600	0.000	0.000
Percent of property tax deductible (γ)	0.600	0.000	0.000
Loan-to-value ratio (β)	0.400	0.400	0.400
P_H	1.000	1.000	1.170
Percent of interest income taxable (e)	0.500	0.500	0.000

correspondingly. The final row of table 4–A1 shows a parameter indicating the fraction of capital income subject to tax (e). We choose a preform value of $e = 0.5$, a choice based on Engen and Gale (1996), which reflects the widespread existence of tax-preferred saving vehicles that permit substantial amounts of interest (and other capital income) to escape income taxation. Because the flat tax would eliminate taxation of capital income, e falls to zero.

Notes

1.   DRI estimates the value of the mortgage interest ($62 billion) and property tax ($22 billion) deductions at $84 billion annually. With a real discount rate of 0.05, the value of that in perpetuity would be $1.7 trillion.

2.   As the key to that result, the tax is not levied on existing housing—such an assumption seems sensible. First, the exemption of existing housing is characteristic of most reform proposals. Moreover, if a tax on housing were politically palatable, the current tax benefits for housing would not have survived to this day.

3.   In equilibrium, the purchase price of a house is equal to the present

value of the future consumption stream. Hence, a tax on the purchase price is equivalent to "prepaying" a stream of future taxes on the annual consumption value.

4.   The equivalence between the retail sales tax and the VAT is perhaps most easily seen by viewing the VAT as a multistage collection mechanism for the tax on the final product.

5.   Another possibility is a "consumed income tax" administered entirely at the household level, but political realities appear to preclude this approach. Thus, for example, we do not address the USA tax of Senators Nunn and Domenici.

6.   See Bruce and Holtz-Eakin 1998 for a more detailed description of the numerical simulation model underlying the discussion.

7.   It is traditional to treat the capital gain on housing as effectively untaxed (see, for example, Rosen 1985). The most recent tax bill (the Taxpayer Relief Act of 1997) makes it even more likely that capital gains will not be subjected to a tax.

Equation 4–1 ignores the distinction between equity and mortgage financing costs, assumes that all mortgage interest and property taxes are fully deducted, and assumes that interest income is fully taxable. We can relax these assumptions. Let β denote the loan-to-value ratio (that is, the fraction of the house value that is mortgaged), Θ the portion of financing costs that are deductible, γ the fraction of property taxes that are deductible, and e the portion of interest income that is taxable. Then the expression becomes

$$i[\beta(1 - \Theta\tau) + (1 - \beta)(1 - e\tau)] = \frac{\left[\dfrac{S(H)}{H} + t_p(1 - \gamma\tau) + \delta + m\right]P_H}{P_H} + \frac{\Delta P_H}{P_H}.$$

This more exact expression is used in our numerical computations.

8.   Both choices ensure revenue neutrality. See the appendix to this chapter.

9.   Many observers feel that supply responses in the housing market are asymmetric—increases are more elastic than contractions in supply. Our simulations focus exclusively on scenarios that result in a decline in the stock of housing, and our elasticities are best interpreted in this context.

See Bruce and Holtz-Eakin (1998) for a detailed summary of the sensitivity analysis.

10.   The steady-state values are computed by setting $\Delta P_H = 0$, determining the long-run value of P_H, and solving for the corresponding value of H.

11.   The situation implies a price rise to purchasers but no net gain to builders.

12.   Those results are consistent with the findings in static, general equilibrium analyses of housing. Berkovec and Fullerton (1992) estimate that the removal of the deduction for mortgage interest (property tax) would reduce the stock of housing by 2.6 (2.1) percent. Nakagami and Pereira (1996) find that removing the deduction for mortgage interest would reduce housing wealth by less than 1 percent.

13. Our simulations do not incorporate the existence of the standard deduction and thus overstate the loss from the removal of deductions.

14. Again, the net-of-tax price of new housing would initially decline; the incentive is exactly what is required to induce a contraction in the supply of housing.

References

Berkovec, James, and Don Fullerton. 1992. "A General Equilibrium Model of Housing, Taxes, and Portfolio Choice." *Journal of Political Economy* 100(2): 390–429.

Besley, Timothy J., and Harvey S. Rosen. 1998. "Sales Taxes and Prices: An Empirical Analysis." National Bureau of Economic Research Working Paper 6667. Cambridge: NBER, July.

Brinner, Roger, Mark Lansky, and David Wyss. 1995. "Market Impacts of Flat Tax Legislation." *DRI/McGraw-Hill U.S. Review,* June.

Bruce, Donald, and Douglas Holtz-Eakin. 1998. "Apocalypse Now? Fundamental Tax Reform and Residential Housing Values." Mimeo. Syracuse: Syracuse University.

Capozza, Dennis R., Richard K. Green, and Patric H. Hendershott. 1996. "Taxes, Mortgage Borrowing, and Residential Land Prices." In *Economic Effects of Fundamental Tax Reform,* edited by Henry J. Aaron and William G. Gale: Washington, D.C.: Brookings Institution Press.

Engen, Eric, and William Gale. 1996. "The Effects of Fundamental Tax Reform on Saving." In *Economic Effects of Fundamental Tax Reform,* edited by Henry J. Aaron and William G. Gale. Washington, D.C.: Brookings Institution Press.

Follain, James R,. and Lisa Sturman Melamed. 1998. "The False Messiah of Tax Policy: What Elimination of the Home Mortgage Interest Deduction Promises and a Careful Look at What It Delivers." *Journal of Housing Research* 9 (2): 179–99.

Gale, William. 1997. "What Can America Learn from the British Tax System?" Mimeo. Washington, D.C.: Brookings Institution.

Hall, Robert, and Alvin Rabushka. 1995. *The Flat Tax.* 2d ed. Stanford, Calif.: Hoover Institution Press.

Nakagami, Yasuhiro, and Alfredo M. Pereira. 1996. "Budgetary and Efficiency Effects of Housing Taxation in the United States." *Journal of Urban Economics* 39 (1): 68–86.

Rosen, Harvey S. 1985. "Housing Subsidies: Effects on Housing Decisions, Efficiency, and Equity." In *The Handbook of Public Economics,* vol. 1, edited by M. Feldstein and A. Auerbach. Amsterdam: North-Holland.

U.S. Bureau of the Census, 1995. *Statistical Abstract of the United States, 1995.* 115th ed. Washington, D.C.

Commentary

William G. Gale

Bruce and Holtz-Eakin have produced one of the few fully integrated analyses of a topic that generates tremendous controversy. The underlying model provides a rigorous analysis of how fundamental tax reform would affect the housing market. By integrating housing supply and demand and linking the transitional and long-term impacts of tax reform, the model allows the consideration of reforms under constant and plausible conditions.

The authors decompose the shift from the current tax system to a broad-based consumption tax into two parts: (1) a shift from the current system to a broad-based income tax and (2) a shift from a broad-based income tax to a broad-based consumption tax. The first change is captured by removing deductions for mortgage interest and property taxes. The second change is captured by removing taxes on interest income and by modeling a consumption tax with a base including the sale of newly constructed housing, but not sales of already existing housing. It is easiest to follow the results if the consumption tax is thought of as a national retail sales tax, and I use the terms interchangeably here. Nevertheless, all results and intuition would remain the same if the consumption tax took some other form.

My comments on the specifics of the model focus on three issues: (1) the analysis of the effects of removing deductions for mortgage interest and property taxes; (2) the appropriate interpretation of changes in housing prices when shifting from a broad-based income tax to a broad-based consumption tax; and (3) the absence of consideration of effects on land prices. In each case, I believe that the model is overly optimistic regarding the impact of tax reform on housing.

Effects of Removing Deductions. Moving to a broad-based income tax by removing the deductions for mortgage interest and property taxes has small effects in the model: housing demand is modeled as a function of the characteristics of the typical homeowner, and only about 40 percent of homeowners itemize their deductions. The market value (selling price) of a house, however, is what a buyer is willing to pay for it, less any taxes and transaction costs. Therefore, the demand for housing should depend on the characteristics of, and deductions taken by, the typical buyer. My guess is that the typical buyer, relative to the typical owner, is more likely to take on a mortgage, have a high loan-to-value ratio, and itemize deductions. If these conjectures are correct, removing the deductions would have a more negative effect on housing prices and quantity than the model indicates.

Interpreting Changes in Housing Prices under a Consumption Tax. To analyze the shift from a broad-based income tax to a broad-based sales tax

requires a consistent set of assumptions about how the producer and consumer price levels adjust. The authors assume that the shift to a consumption
tax would leave the producer price level constant and would raise the consumer price level (including the sales tax) by the full amount of the sales tax.
Under this assumption, the break-even selling price of a newly constructed
home rises to $1+t$ under the sales tax, from a level of 1 under the income tax,
where t is the tax-exclusive sales tax rate.[1] Since new and old houses are the
same product to a consumer, the price of old houses must also rise to $1+t$
from 1. As a result, the after-tax nominal value of old housing, which would
be exempt under the consumption tax, would rise relative to newly constructed housing, which would be taxed under the consumption tax.

The key point, however, is that the after-tax value of old housing would not
rise in value *relative to other consumption goods.* That is, adjusted for changes
in the consumer price level, the after-tax value of existing housing would
remain constant. Assume that, before tax reform, all houses cost $100,000
and the consumer price index (CPI) = 1. After the imposition of a 17 percent
sales tax, the CPI, including the consumption tax, would be 1.17, under the
authors' assumption that the sales tax would be passed forward to consumers,
and existing houses would sell for $117,000. Because the sale of an already
existing house would not be taxed, the seller of an existing house would keep
the entire $117,000 (ignoring transactions costs). But $117,000 in cash after
the sales tax was implemented would buy only as much in consumption
goods as $100,000 in cash before the sales tax. Thus, the real value of old
houses relative to other consumption goods would not have changed, even
though the nominal price of old housing would have increased by 17 percent.

This finding has crucial implications for the model and results. First, if the
real value of old housing remains constant relative to other consumption
goods, but rises relative to the value of new housing, the real value of new
housing must fall relative to other consumption goods.

Second, all price changes resulting from a shift to a consumption tax
reported in table 4–1 and figures 4–2, 4–4, 4–6, and 4–7 represent nominal
changes based on the assumption that switching to a consumption tax would
raise the consumer price level by the full amount of the tax. To obtain the
changes in real prices, all those results must be reduced by seventeen percentage points. That adjustment has a dramatic impact on the interpretation
of the results.

In the long run, the reported nominal price change of 17 percent in
table 4C–1 represents a real change of zero in housing prices. That is consistent with the authors' assumption that the cost of building a house would stay
constant over time. Indeed, that long-term outcome is the only one consistent with the constant costs of replacement and competition in the housing
industry.

In the short run, the effects of the reinterpretation are equally important.
For example, the transition results for the baseline case in figure 4–2 indicate

TABLE 4C–1
Effects on Housing Prices from Shift to a Consumption Tax
(in percent)

	One-Year Effects		Long-Run Effects	
	Producer prices constant after tax reform	Producer prices fallen after tax reform	Producer prices constant after tax reform	Producer prices fallen after tax reform
Real prices of structures	- 6	-6	0	0
Nominal prices of structures	+11	-6	+17	0

that nominal house prices would rise by about 11 percent in the first year after conversion to a consumption tax. By implication, real house prices would fall by about 6 percent because the consumer price level would rise by 17 percent. By similar logic, the example of a low-supply response in figure 4–4 implies a real drop in house prices of about 8 percent in year 1 and a decline of 4 percent after four years. The worst-case scenario in figure 4–6 implies a real price decline of about 28 percent after one year and about 17 percent after seven years. Even ten years after tax reform, the implied real price decline would be about 7 percent.

Nothing guarantees, of course, that a shift to a consumption tax would hold the producer price level constant and would raise consumer prices. In a polar alternative scenario, producer prices would fall by the full amount of the removed income tax, so that the consumer price level (including the consumption tax) after tax reform would equal the consumer price level before tax reform. Under this scenario, the change in real house prices would be the same as noted above. In the long run, nominal housing prices would be constant, rather than rising 17 percent. In year 1 (in the baseline case in figure 4–2), nominal housing prices would fall by 6 percent, rather than rising by 11 percent. Table 4C–1 summarizes the various alternatives for changes in price levels and changes in real and nominal house prices.[2]

The Role of Land. The chapter equates owner-occupied housing with housing structures, but housing is really a composite good consisting of a structure and land. The structure is a produced good and has a finite life. In the extreme, land is a pure natural resource with an infinite life. Of course, in practice this extreme definition may not hold: cleared land is a produced good, and the quality of land may deteriorate over time. Nevertheless, for practical purposes, it is worthwhile to think of housing as consisting of two goods that may have different characteristics and different responses to tax policy.

The authors included land in prior work and found that it had only a small effect on the outcome. They found that land prices would fall by about 2 percent in the years immediately following conversion to a consumption tax and in the long run would rise by 17 percent. However, those figures represent nominal price changes in a model that assumes that consumer prices would rise by the full amount of the consumption tax. Thus, the implied real price change was -19 percent in the first few years and zero in the long run.

Effects of this magnitude should not be surprising. The present value of land that yields an income of $1 per year forever is $1/r$, where r is the after-tax interest rate. In the authors' model, the after-tax interest rate rises from 5.85 percent (= .075*(1 - 0.22)) under the income tax to 7.5 percent under the consumption tax. The shift should reduce real land prices by 22 percent, with other factors held constant.

The inclusion of the effect of tax reform on land prices can affect both the short-run and long-run impact of tax reform on housing. Data from the flow of funds indicate that in 1998, land was about 25 percent of the total value of residential structures plus land. Thus, in the short run, a 22 percent decline in the real value of land, coupled with a 6 percent real drop in the value of structures (taken from the baseline scenario in figure 4-2), would suggest a drop in the value of housing (structures and land) equal to 10 percent (= 0.25* 0.22 + 0.75*0.06).

In the long run, any increase in the after-tax interest rate would reduce the value of land. Thus, even if the long-run value of structures remained constant as the authors have assumed, the long-run price of housing (structures plus land) would be expected to fall if the after-tax interest rate rose because of tax reform. For example, if the after-tax interest rate rose from 5.85 percent to 7.5 percent as the authors assume, the real price of housing (structures plus land) would fall by about 5.5 percent (= 0.25*0.22 +0 .75*0) in the long run. If the real after-tax rate rose to only 6.5 percent, land would fall by 10 percent in value and the real value of housing (structures plus land) would fall by 2.2 percent in the long run.

In summary, the three issues noted above suggest that in a formal, internally consistent model of the housing market with reasonable parameters, fundamental tax reform could easily generate extreme declines in real house value (structures plus land) in the short run and significant declines in the long run. In particular, based on the considerations above, shifting to a consumption tax would reduce the prices of real housing (structure plus land) by about 7–10 percent initially and by about 2–6 percent in the long run, depending on the response of the after-tax interest rate. Although those outcomes and their side effects would not kill the housing market, they merit serious consideration in formulating tax reform options.

Future research extending the model by considering these issues more completely would be interesting. Other areas of interest are the interactions between rental housing markets and the owner-occupied market, as well as further analysis of an issue that the authors mention but do not pursue:

whether and through what channels large and rapid contractions in the supply of owner-occupied housing could occur.

The remainder of my comment focuses on two issues: the impact of changes in house prices and political aspects of removing tax preferences for housing.

Changes in real house prices, even if relatively small, can be large relative to other effects of tax reform. For example, Gale, Houser, and Scholz (1996) find that under the flat tax, 31 percent of all households would face changes in tax burdens of less than 1 percent of income; an additional 54 percent would face changes of 1-5 percent of income. As a rough estimate, let house value equal about 2.5 times income for a typical family, and assume that in the long run, real house prices would fall by 5 percent because of fundamental tax reform. Under these circumstances, the price of housing would fall by 12.5 percent of income, or several times the direct impact of tax reform on annual tax payments. Of course, the change in house prices would be a one-time phenomenon; nonetheless, the example shows that changes in house values can be an important aspect of the effects of changes in tax policy.

Even if real housing prices did not decline, lower nominal housing prices would raise the likelihood of mortgage defaults. The single best predictor of default is whether a household's outstanding loan balance exceeds its housing equity. A reduction in nominal housing prices would reduce housing equity for all households. That situation raises concerns because most outstanding mortgages are relatively new and thus are likely to have a large percentage of loan value still outstanding. By implication, even relatively modest declines in nominal house values could trigger defaults.

A rough calculation provides an example of the potential for this event. Data from the American Housing Survey show that about 47 percent of outstanding mortgages in the mid-1990s were less than five years old.[3] If the interest rate were 8 percent, a borrower would have paid off 5 percent of the principal on a thirty-year mortgage after five years. Finally, assume that half of all new mortgages have loan-to-value ratios of 90 percent or more. Under these assumptions, a tax reform that reduced nominal housing values by 15 percent would place at least 23.5 percent of mortgage holders in a zero or negative equity position. Even if the average impact of tax reform on housing prices was smaller than that, most analysts agree that the effects of tax reform on house prices would vary considerably across areas. Thus, a significant minority of households could find themselves in a negative housing equity position.

The authors also highlight the political problems of removing housing subsidies. A few comments are relevant here. Changes in the value of the deduction for mortgage interest are nothing new. They occur every time interest rates or tax rates change. As a rough calculation, let the value of the deduction for mortgage interest, per dollar of outstanding loan, be given by the marginal tax rate times the mortgage interest rate. With that definition, table

TABLE 4C–2
Value of Mortgage Interest Deduction, 1980 and 1995

Tax Rate Percentile	1980	1995
25th	2.02	1.18
50th	2.66	1.18
75th	3.54	1.18
90th	4.68	2.20
95th	5.44	2.20
99th	6.84	2.83

NOTE: The value of the deduction for mortgage interest is assumed to be the product of the mortgage interest rate times the tax rate. Data on mortgage interest rates are taken from the *Economic Report of the President*. Data on the distribution of marginal tax rates are taken from Burman, Gale, and Weiner 1998.

4C–2 shows that, from 1980 to 1995, the value fell by 50–60 percent for households in the upper half of the income distribution.[4] During this period, both nominal interest rates and marginal tax rates fell significantly.

Moreover, the common assertion that Congress put the deduction for mortgage interest in the tax code to encourage homeownership seems implausible, at best. Deductions for mortgage interest and property taxes were features of the original income tax in 1913, which applied only to the top 1 percent of households. It is difficult to believe that encouraging homeownership among this group was an important public policy goal in 1913.

Nor does the presence of a deduction for mortgage interest seem to affect homeownership rates much across countries. Without that deduction, Canada, for example, has a homeownership rate roughly equal to that in the United States.

Recently, Great Britain conducted a fascinating experiment showing both the political and economic viability of reducing mortgage subsidies.[5] When tax subsidies for most forms of borrowing were eliminated in 1974–1975, subsidies for interest on the principal primary residence were retained, subject to a loan limit of £25,000. No subsidies were provided on second homes. The limit was raised to £30,000 in 1983–1984 and has stayed fixed since. The limit applies to the sum of loans against each property. Mortgage tax relief after 1974 was initially provided at the taxpayer's marginal income tax rate. More recently, the subsidy has been provided only up to a fixed rate, set at 25 percent and then reduced to 15 percent for new loans in 1998.

The British experience raises several interesting possibilities. First, relief for mortgage interest has been effectively divorced from the tax system. The statutory rate of subsidy and the loan limit are independent of marginal tax rates. Second, because the £30,000 limit is well below the average new mortgage loan, mortgage subsidies provide no marginal incentive for most taxpayers. Third, the decline in the value of the mortgage interest subsidy has been gradual, but huge. From 1974 to 1996, the value—thought of as the interest rate times the rate at which the subsidy is taken times the real loan limit—fell by about 90 percent.

Nevertheless, finding much of an effect of the policies on the housing sector is difficult. From 1974 to 1994, homeownership rates, the ratio of mortgage debt to GDP, the ratio of mortgage debt to the housing stock, and the ratio of housing to fixed capital rose faster in the United Kingdom than in the United States. Granted, many other factors affect these trends—the privatization of public housing in Britain in the 1980s being a possible major factor. But the significant reduction in mortgage subsidies when homeownership rates were rising (by thirteen percentage points from 1974 to 1994) may make the events even more remarkable from a political perspective.

The British experience and cross-country evidence that the presence of a deduction for mortgage interest does not greatly influence homeownership rates suggest that the value of subsidies for owner-occupied housing could be reduced under the existing system without significant economic problems. The Bruce and Holtz-Eakin analysis of removing deductions is generally consistent with that result. But the model results, as interpreted above, suggest that fundamental tax reform could have much larger effects.

Notes

1. If a good has a price tag of $100 and a $20 tax is added at the cash register, the tax-exclusive tax rate is 20 percent (20/100). In contrast, the tax-inclusive rate would be 16.7 percent (20/(100+20)).

2. For further analysis of price level changes and tax reform, see Gale et al. 1998.

3. I thank Alex Brill for providing this information.

4. Bruce and Holtz-Eakin note that the value of the deduction should be adjusted downward to account for the fact that only interest payments in excess of the standard deduction provide tax benefits. However, the value of the deduction should also be adjusted upward to account for the fact that if interest payments do exceed the standard deduction, there is an added tax benefit: charitable contributions, state and local tax payments, and other items also become tax deductible. Thus, measuring the value of the deduction as the tax rate times the interest rate, as in table 4-3, may be a reasonable approcimation.

5. See Gale 1997 for further discussion.

References

Burman, Leonard E., William G. Gale, and David Weiner. 1998. "Six Tax Laws Later: How Individuals' Marginal Federal Income Tax Rates Changed between 1980 and 1995." *National Tax Journal* 51 (3) (September): 637–52.

Gale, William G. 1997. "What Can Americans Learn from the British Tax System?" *National Tax Journal* 50 (4) (December) and *Fiscal Studies* 18 (4) (November): 341–69.

Gale, William G., Scott Houser, and John Karl Scholz. 1996. "Distributional Effects of Fundamental Tax Reform." *In Economic Effects of Fundamental Tax Reform,* edited by Henry J. Aaron and William G. Gale. Washington, D.C.: Brookings Institution.

Gale, William G., Evan F. Koenig, Diane Lim Rogers, and John Sabelhaus. 1998. "Taxing Government in a National Retail Sales Tax." *Tax Notes,* October 5: 97–109.

Index

www.ingramcontent.com/pod-product-compliance
Lightning Source LLC
Jackson TN
JSHW011940131224
75386JS00041B/1468